Praise for *SOAR Selling*

"Our organization experienced an immediate 100 percent ROI from implementing the *SOAR Selling* techniques, but the individual and management accountability standards we gained as a result of the program . . . Priceless!"
—Jeanne B. Jambor, Chief/EVP, Real Capital Analytics

"*SOAR Selling* offers a proven method that will differentiate you from the rest of the pack."
—Jay D. Cimo, Director of Operations, Midwest Brokerage, Jones Lang LaSalle

"As a former National Sales Instructor and then National Sales Support Manager supporting 380 sales professionals with Xerox Canada, I found the SOAR program to be one of the most transformative and influential sales programs to drive new prospects and accelerate sales cycles."
—Lana Verran, Former National Sales Instructor, Xerox Canada

Every salesperson needs to improve his or her prospecting techniques, and our organization has found that *SOAR Selling* offers a proven methodology that will differentiate you. *SOAR Selling* techniques are practical, relevant, and easy to apply. *SOAR Selling* is essential for any professional or organization committed to sales excellence."
—Rich Diaz, President, Advanced Resource Group

"*SOAR Selling* can help you gain access to the people you need to connect with."
—Mike Bosworth, author of *Solution Selling*, and coauthor of *What Great Salespeople Do*

"*SOAR Selling* is a mission-critical tool for building lasting, profitable relationships. David and Marhnelle go far beyond defining a sales process by rolling up their sleeves to share their secret about what you absolutely must do to 'get in' anywhere."
—Marcus Buckingham, *New York Times* bestselling author, researcher, motivational speaker and business consultant

SOAR SELLING

How To Get Through to Almost Anyone —
the Proven Method for Reaching
Decision Makers

DAVID HIBBARD
MARHNELLE HIBBARD

New York   Chicago   San Francisco   Lisbon
London   Madrid   Mexico City   Milan   New Delhi
San Juan   Seoul   Singapore   Sydney   Toronto

Copyright © 2013 by Dialexis. All rights reserved. Printed in the United States of America. Except as permitted under the United States Copyright Act of 1976, no part of this publication may be reproduced or distributed in any form or by any means, or stored in a database or retrieval system, without the prior written permission of the publisher.

1 2 3 4 5 6 7 8 9 10   DOC/DOC   1 8 7 6 5 4 3 2

ISBN 978-0-07-179371-1
MHID   0-07-179371-2

e-ISBN 978-0-07-179372-8
e-MHID   0-07-179372-0

Library of Congress Cataloging-in-Publication Data

Hibbard, David.
    SOAR selling : how to get through to almost anyone : the proven method for reaching decision makers / by David Hibbard and Marhnelle Hibbard.
        p. cm
    ISBN-13: 978-0-07-179371-1 (alk. paper)
    ISBN-10: 0-07-179371-2 (alk. paper)
1. Selling. I. Hibbard, Marhnelle S. II. Title.
    HF5438.25.H53 2013
    658.85—dc23

                                                              2012033479

DiSC is a registered trademark of Inscape Publishing.

McGraw-Hill books are available at special quantity discounts to use as premiums and sales promotions or for use in corporate training programs. To contact a representative, please e-mail us at bulksales@mcgraw-hill.com.

This book is printed on acid-free paper.

CONTENTS

Why SOAR?

The power of SOAR has been tracked by numerous corporations throughout North America and Europe. Consistently, the results yielded stunning return on investment (ROI): our clients have reported an ROI ranging from 200 percent to 2,000 percent on their initial investment over a 12-week period!

That is quite substantial when you think about it. An organization's sales force receives the training and, within 12 weeks, actualizes an explosive ROI . . . imagine what *a year* of SOAR performance could do. (For those organizations where their sale cannot close in 12 weeks, Dialexis uses an assumed ROI based upon the pipeline produced using SOAR.)

SOAR Selling is a set of proven tactics sales professionals can use to make contact with decision makers and high influencers during cold prospecting that result in up to 90 percent contact on every net dial. For the first time, this book reveals the entire SOAR strategy. We can tell you right now that SOAR won't support you if you just read it and employ it in a haphazard fashion; reading about exercise does not make you healthier. For SOAR to have benefit, you have to be open to its powerful potential to change your results and move you to the Top 20 percent+ and keep you there. One way to get to the Top 20 percent+ and stay there is to continually drive *net new business . . . demand generation* is the path.

Though the fundamentals remain rock solid, SOAR is a formula and its power is enhanced by every obstacle overcome and every success story realized. Throughout our years of developing and training SOAR, there have been times when salespeople and their managers were still questioning SOAR validity, right up to the moment of live dialing in a corporate training class.

Once the live dialing took place (calls made by the attendees themselves), the reality of SOAR was accepted. Completing live net new dials in class during the training is something our attendees do in each and every SOAR program.

Although we can't make *live dials* through this book, what we can do is point out the importance of a positive *mindset* and give you the fundamentals: the systematic winning formula SOAR utilizes. The secret to making contact with decision makers at an amazing level is outlined for you in the following pages. Put it into practice and track your own results, and when you do, please go to the SOAR website at www.soarselling.com and click on the tab "SOAR wins". . . to share your success stories!

ACKNOWLEDGMENTS

This book would not have been published if it were not for my life and business partner Marhnelle, who is coauthor of this work, and Shelley Harriger, who has been with Dialexis from the beginning. Both pushed and pushed to get this information in written format. As a result, it has had an immense impact on many salespeople who have struggled making *net new contact* with corporate executives. Lives have been changed, spirits have been lifted, money has been made, families have been impacted, and in my view, the world is better because of SOAR. Thanks also to every individual who has made suggestions and contributed in one way or another to make SOAR what it has become today, with special appreciation Michael Bosworth, Dale Stein, Mark Goulston and our supportive family.

—David Hibbard

I would like to thank all of those individuals who were courageous enough to sit in the "hot seat" making *live net new calls* in front of others! It was because of your results that this book was written. I would also like to thank my friend and trusted colleague Shelley Harriger for her commitment to SOAR and Dialexis along with Gabriel Nossovitch for his work and pledge to transformation development. In addition, I would also like to thank master trainer Frank Cook for his contribution in refining SOAR, Mark Goulston for his generosity, Michael Bosworth for his support, Dale Stein for always being there for us, and all the trainers who deliver SOAR so powerfully each day. I would also like to thank the trainers that have enhanced this work and have supported so many individuals in their quest to create superior results. To my mom, Lorene—you are my inspiration, living life to the fullest and always open to new possibilities. My sister and nieces and last, but never least I would like to thank my extraordinary family Ticole, Tydus, Blair, Matt, Rob, Dorothy, Chloe, Luke, Major, Sloane, Zane and my husband and amazing partner, you have always been my inspiration and encouragement.

—**Marhnelle Hibbard**

SOAR
SELLING

WHAT IS SOAR?

What Is SOAR?

SOAR is a contact formula created by Dialexis for reaching decision makers and high influencers on the telephone. SOAR stands for *Surge of Accelerating Revenue*. The SOAR program supports salespeople from any industry to make *fewer* net new business development dials while making a *higher* percentage of contacts and appointments.

SOAR evolved from extensive field research conducted by David and Marhnelle Hibbard, the Dialexis sales team, and the Dialexis training field team. A period of over 15 years was devoted to the development of the SOAR strategy. Making contact with decision makers and high influencers is a formidable task, one that required a multitude of approaches to find a successful solution. We were determined to develop a formula that would yield a contact rate that would revolutionize the way salespeople make contact over the phone.

As we tested various approaches over the years, one thing we focused on consistently was finding a solution that was ethical and instructional and that anyone could execute. Once we believed we had the formula, we tested the approach throughout the United States, Canada, and central and eastern Europe. We received rave reviews from corporate leaders, sales managers, and salespeople alike. Organizations that experienced SOAR expressed amazement not only at how well the techniques worked, but were equally impressed at the measured ROI (return on investment) numbers that SOAR drove over such a short period. Through SOAR, senior sales professionals and rookies alike began to experience a new way of prospecting for net new business. Organizations implementing SOAR penetrated a multitude of blockades, ultimately making contact with up to 90 percent of every net dial. When combined with accountability, a measurable ROI in the range of 200 to 2,000 percent was achieved in as little as 12 weeks from program inception.

Today, organizations throughout the world, such as Vistage, CoStar, Oracle, Cisco, AT&T, AOL, Dell, Los Angeles Angels of Anaheim, Morgan Stanley, Berlin, PGi, Yahoo! and hundreds of smaller entrepreneurial firms have introduced SOAR to their sales force and have experienced the new way executive contact can be made using the telephone.

How SOAR Differentiates

Other sales training philosophies focus on *what to do once you get in*. We realized that the prevailing problem facing salespeople was *how to get in*. Salespeople needed a way to get past blockades and into the "exclusive club" of decision makers without making hundreds of calls. Various successful selling programs like SPIN Selling, Sandler Selling, PSS, Solution Selling, and Strategic Selling are all top-notch, but they focus on what to do once a salesperson gets in. We decided that if we could solve the problem of *how* to get in, we could make a salesperson's life easier, provide a better solution for driving net new business, and, at the same time, reduce attrition for corporations because salespeople would now have a method for making contact.

Here are the key advantages that SOAR provides:

- **Contact.** SOAR provides a quantifiable contact rate with decision makers and high influencers of up to 90 percent on every net dial to a new prospect. Again, other vendors focus on what to do once the salesperson gets in . . . SOAR is all about *how to get in*. The 90 percent contact rate statistic is the current number, and it is updated quarterly with actual numbers from live trainings.

- **ROI.** The program is measurable. Organizations have experienced a 200 to 2,000 percent ROI 12 weeks from program completion (the vast range from 200 to 2,000 percent is due to an organization's or individual's value statement, which we will address later.) Simply stated, when a client makes an investment with SOAR and executes on that investment, they can expect to receive from 200 to 2,000 percent ROI in 12 weeks!

- **Accountability.** With SOAR, managers and salespeople are accountable for results during the 12-week measurement period. Dialexis interfaces with the leaders involved in the program consistently on a schedule during this time frame. Essentially, the coaching segment of SOAR allows Dialexis to stay with the client for the 12-week tracking period to ensure the program consistently demonstrates revenue surge and ROI.

- **Tactics and Mindset.** Dialexis understands that tactics matter, but also realizes the importance of mindset. As a result, Dialexis has included a mindset component in all its training programs. It's not simply *how to do a something* that makes the difference, but *why*. The mindset segment sets up the individual to be open to a new way of approaching driving net new business using the SOAR formula.

- **Proof of Concept.** Dialexis teaches how to reach decision makers live on the telephone (or on the streets, which is an entirely different approach), then has the sales group make live calls in the class demonstrating they can execute the SOAR formula. In most instances, every single attendee dials live in front of the class with the instructor present and coaching. With Dialexis, once the instructor leaves, it is assured that the training works and attendees can execute what they learned.

- **Train the Trainer.** For the Fortune 500 companies or organizations with a substantial number of salespeople, Dialexis has developed a train the trainer deliverable. Any corporate nominated individual wishing to be certified in the SOAR methodology can do so. This subsequently reduces the overall financial investment for the client and speeds up the delivery of the information to the field.

- **Reputation.** As we mentioned earlier, SOAR has demonstrated its effectiveness with a multitude of Fortune 500 organizations as well as many mid-size to smaller entrepreneurial firms.

ROI and Measurement

Let's take a look at one powerful example of SOAR's efficacy. Dialexis was retained by a Fortune 500 company in 2007 with a strong brand to provide SOAR training to a team of salespeople who were primarily compensated on commission. The client requested a pilot program to evaluate its potential to drive top line revenue through net new business. The candidates selected for the training varied from rookie to mid-level to highly experienced. If the SOAR program was a success, the client would be able to roll out the program throughout the United States. In preprogram discussions, the client agreed that ROI was critical in order to demonstrate to upper management that the investment in time and money was a wise one. The training was completed in three days in Southern California with key managers in attendance and measured over a post 12-week period, as is standard with SOAR. All results were tracked and strictly validated by the client, while Dialexis coached and monitored.

Participants in the pilot program were measuring their SOAR dials using a contact management system maintained by the client. Through this system, they were able to validate that all SOAR dials (new business development calls) were tracked and authentic. The objective was to reach decision makers and C-level high influencers over the 12-week period. All metric results were turned over to the local sales managers and subsequently provided to Dialexis for statistical evaluation. Over the period of 12 weeks, all managers and the Dialexis team were on coaching/analysis calls, discussing results.

The final verified tabulated metrics are shown in the following overview in Figures 1-1 to 1-4. (See definition of key terms in Figure 1-1 below.) These are *real results*. Ask yourself, if you were to drive net new business like the examples in this study, where would your organization (and personal income) be? Where would you rank with your peers? Where would you be spending the next holiday vacation with your family? You may want to reread these metrics and remind yourself again that salespeople just like you created the results shown.

SOAR world stats →	100	40%	60%	46%	44%	Contact		88%		20% 30%				
Sales team	Dial goal	Gross dials	N/A	Net dials	DM	HI	Total	Contact rate %	% of goal	Total appt.	Appt. %	Projected revenue	Closed revenue	% Closed to proj. rev.
Team 1	5208	4428	2408	2020	716	1030	1746	86%	85%	289	14%	$875,000	$346,000	39.5%
Team 2	4678	3543	1695	1848	524	786	1310	71%	76%	228	12%	$705,000	$205,000	29.1%
Total	9886	7971	4103	3868	1240	1816	3056	79%	81%	517	13%	$1,580,000	$551,000	34.9%

Final 12 week gross ROI = 1867.86%
Final 12 week net ROI = 589.29%

Definitions

- **Dials:** Reflects the number of *gross* dials made in the program
- **N/A:** Reflects the non-applicable calls (such as wrong numbers, fax lines, etc.)
- **NET:** Reflects N/A's less dials or *net* dials
- **DM:** Reflects the % of decision maker contacts (against net dials)
- **HI:** Reflects the % of high influencer C-level contacts (against net dials)
- **Appt:** Reflects the % of appointments against net dials

Figure 1-1 *Case Study: Fortune 500 Company Final 12-Week SOAR Total Results Net New Calls*

Managers	Goal: 15 net dials	Gross dials	NA	Net dials	Contact DM	Contact HI	Total contacts	Appts. scheduled	Appts. completed	MRR pipeline	Annualized pipeline	Closed MRR	Closed annual $
Manager		2063	913	1150	474	633	1107	196	136	$40,004	$480,048	$1,973	$23,676
Manager		3084	1524	1560	390	710	1100	318	293	$41,178	$494,136	$14,483	$173,796
Manager		2678	1174	1504	571	869	1440	158	100	$25,462	$305,542	$4,514	$54,168
Manager		2203	1140	1063	325	701	1026	159	122	$33,187	$398,244	$14,699	$176,388
Manager		2454	669	1785	608	807	1415	113	65	$59,780	$717,360	$9,265	$111,180
Totals	10,020	12,482	5,420	7,062	2,368	3,720	6,088	944	716	$199,611	$2,395,330	$44,934	$539,208
Client %		43% ⇕		33% ⇕	53% ⇕	86% ⇕	13% ⇕				↑		↑
SOAR U.S. stats %		40%		46%	44%	90%	20%+						

12 week *annualized* gross ROI = 1697.36%

Assuming a 20% close rate on what is still in the pipeline; SOAR would provide an additional **$479,066** in annual bookings giving a total assumed gross ROI of **3294.25%**

Definitions

- **Gross dials:** Each time a salesperson attempts to make a call
- **N/A:** Reflects the non-applicable calls. (Dial doesn't count because of: 1. *Wrong number,* 2. *No answer,* 3. *Lost in technology, can't get back to operator,* 4. *Rode the bull four times and hung up due to the operator becoming annoyed.* 5. *No one was in that day.*)
- **NET:** The number of gross dials less N/A's
- **DM:** Decision makers C-level execs
- **HI:** High influencer (EAP) and other key influencers
- **Appointment scheduled:** Total number of appointments set with either DM or HI
- Appointment percentage is calculated against net dials

Figure 1-2 *SOAR 12-Week Tracking Results*

SOAR results control group comparison

SAE performance with SOAR vs. SAE performance without SOAR
June 1–August 14, 2009

Non-SOAR closes – Outbound program rankings (control group)		SOAR closes – Outbound program rankings	
Account executive	MRR	Account executive	MRR
1 Rep D	$4,015	1 Rep F	$11,536
2 Rep V	$3,628	2 Rep Q	$8,265
3 Rep J	$2,935	3 Rep M	$7,426
4 Rep T	$2,125	4 Rep M	$3,720
5 Rep K	$2,122	5 Rep L	$3,163
6 Rep R	$2,050	6 Rep L	$2,107
7 Rep S	$1,700	7 Rep P	$2,105
8 Rep D	$1,478	8 Rep A	$2,100
9 Rep B	$1,447	9 Rep R	$1,704
10 Rep C	$1,170	10 Rep L	$1,037
11 M Rep	$875	11 Rep J	$1,000
12 Rep T	$411	12 Rep P	$302
13 Rep M	$20	13 Rep R	$269
14 Rep D	$0	14 Rep S	$200
Non SOAR total	(Per month) $23,976	SOAR total	(Per month) $44,934

**SOAR™ increased annualized
closed revenue by**
$251,496 (+87.41%)

Figure 1-3 *SOAR Results Control Group SAE*

SOAR results comparison

SAE performance with SOAR vs. SAE performance without SOAR
June 1–August 14, 2009

Non-SOAR closes – Outbound program rankings (control group)	SOAR closes – Outbound program rankings
Average deal size: $359 Average days to close: 19.5	Average deal size: $607 (+69%) Average days to close: 9.4 (−52%)

Key accomplishments:

➤ **1697% gross ROI** on the initial SOAR investment 12 weeks from inception

➤ **Time to close a transaction decreased** by over 10 days (**52% decrease**)

➤ Average **deal size increased** by over $248 (**69% increase**)

➤ **Increased confidence** to have C-level conversations

➤ **SOAR team sold 87% more** than a comparison non-SOAR team with more tenure

SOAR increased annualized
closed revenue by
$251,496 (+87%)

Figure 1-4 *Final Numbers & Results from SAE Control Group Study*

What People Are Saying About SOAR

Sales Manager: "First, let me say that this approach to calling was a first for me. I have been through numerous trainings over the years that all focused on what to say and do once you are engaged with the decision maker. None has focused on how to get to the decision maker. I know that our management team has sat through hundreds of interviews where every candidate talks about their ability to get to the C-level decision makers and close deals—but few are truly doing this effectively. The SOAR program proved that getting to C-level decision makers is not as hard as we have made it out to be. The initial training session where we did live calls was the icing on the cake. We saw SOAR working on live calls in front of the reps' peer groups over and over again. I will use this approach for the rest of my selling career. Thank You."

VP of Sales: "This was a real confidence builder for the reps. Now they have the confidence they can get the same results (or better) from calling current customers or noncustomers. No hesitation on making noncustomer calls now."

Salesperson: "I liked the aggressive call approach that helps you make the most out of your prospecting time. Although you make fewer dials, you are making contact as well as gathering the information you need and discover who the *right* decision maker is at the company."

Salesperson: "This course is an excellent source of inspiration for getting out and selling. I think it taught me more about what to do than anything else I've seen. I liked the tips, the interaction, the energy, and the overall lesson. I especially liked the emphasis on total self-improvement which I will carry over into all other facets of my life."

Salesperson: "SOAR is a very objective and logical tool that all sales reps and nonsales reps could profit from. The experience was fun! Identifying the obstacles and having the tools to use to get through the defenses of the receptionist world is awesome."

Eliminating the Old Way of Prospecting

Whether you've been in sales for 20 years or 2 weeks you've probably experienced someone telling you that the way to prospect on the telephone is based on "BTN + L" (By The Numbers + Luck). Essentially, what this tells salespeople is to just make lots of calls and they will eventually make contact and get an appointment, that is, get lucky. (It's considered to be a truth in sales that if you throw enough against the wall, something will stick.) The problem with the BTN + L approach is that it actually creates less interest in prospecting, promotes unethical performance, and, ultimately, leads to more attrition. Salespeople already hate the task of prospecting; when someone says, "just make a lots of calls and you will eventually make contact," it should come as no surprise that salespeople avoid prospecting like the plague.

Another consequence of BTN + L is the proliferation of articles stating that calling cold doesn't work. The truth is that calling cold doesn't work the BTN + L way—but it *does* work the SOAR way. We're not saying that salespeople now love to prospect because of SOAR; we're just saying that demand generation is at least tolerable. As we said earlier, if salespeople want to reach 10 contacts in a day, they will only have to dial approximately 12 times with SOAR. A method like BTN + L, on the other hand, requires a salesperson to dial often up to 100 times. That's a huge difference in the number of calls required to get a satisfactory result.

We recently talked to a former CEO, now in the recruiting business, who told us that he had made 60 net dials to make 6 contacts. When you do the math, this means he has a dial-to-contact rate of 10 percent. He was definitely using the BTN + L approach! If he had been using the SOAR formula, he would have made approximately 53 fewer net dials to get the same result. Looking at it from another perspective, if the former CEO made the same number of net dials (60), he would have made approximately 54 contacts. (See Glossary of Terms on *net* and *gross* dials at the back of the book.)

Industries that SOAR

We are often asked, "where does SOAR fit best?" The answer is, with any industry or organization that has salespeople that are required to find net new business. Some of the industries who have invited SOAR into their firms are the commercial real estate industry, technology, gaming, building, hospitality, banking, finance, manufacturing, professional services, residential real estate, professional sports, direct marketing, and many additional industries. Organizations within these industries typically had a demand generation initiative or wanted to create a sales culture focused on driving net new business.

If a sales team has to find net new business, SOAR is a great partner. Of course, when it comes to business development there are lots of ways to get the job done; we realize that prospecting by telephone using SOAR is just one way. We understand that networking, relationships, leads groups, club memberships, journals, street prospecting, social media, key account responsibility, and so forth are all viable alternatives to picking up the telephone. It's simply a matter of preference. What's interesting is that demand generation by telephone is often overlooked since it's deemed archaic. Look on the Internet and you will find topics like "Eliminate cold calling," "How to generate warm leads," or "Telephone cold calling doesn't work." With the emergence of the Internet and technology, it seems that cold prospecting on the telephone is a lost art . . . but we know it's still a lethal strategy if done correctly.

Applying SOAR Outside the Sales Environment

The following are two true stories I used that prove SOAR is so effective it can be implemented in almost any situation.

One year, Marhnelle and I were celebrating our anniversary and I decided to surprise her with a trip to Las Vegas to see a hot new show. Since it was going to be a special evening, I wanted to get the best seats I could at a particular casino. I asked a person in our organization to see what was possible. She found tickets at $250 per seat, but the seats were average at best—not at all what I wanted. Since the best seating was in Section A, I suggested she ask about those seats. She did, and was told Section A was not available. Next, we called American Express; we had a special contact there and thought that they would surely have influence. They said they did not have seats in Section A. Instead, they offered seats for $850. They were better than the $250 seats, but still not in Section A! Section A was front and center, and it seemed no one had access to those seats.

We concluded that Section A seats were held by the casino for those "special people" who were high rollers or connected to someone powerful. I decided to use SOAR. Long story short, we ended up with seats in Row 5, Section A, a limo pickup at the Airport, a VIP room, and VIP reservations at a favorite restaurant of the casino's CEO—all for $250! Incidentally, I didn't lie, bend the truth and say I was a big gambler, exaggerate, or misrepresent myself in any way. The SOAR approach really can be used in any situation.

Here is an additional story. The air conditioner in our newly built one-year-old home stopped functioning, so I called the contractor. He immediately sent the crew that originally installed the product. They looked it over and said the coils were salt damaged due to the ocean and would have to be replaced. I asked if the cost of replacing the coils was covered under warranty. They said yes. However, the labor wasn't covered. I pressed further. I didn't understand why I would have to pay for a labor charge. But all they said was that it was just how the manufacturer warranties the unit.

I decided to use SOAR to reach the manufacturer's executive group. It worked. After delivering a compelling value statement, I ended up with the installation of new coils and zero labor cost! I didn't get angry or misrepresent in any way. The key was reaching someone who had the power to make a decision and do the right thing. (In this case, the company was York, and I am pleased to endorse them and their attitude when it comes to taking care of customers.)

The bottom line is that SOAR works for any salesperson wanting to make contact with decision makers or high influencers, and it works just as well for any individual who needs to make contact with someone at the top in order to obtain a desired result. If anyone wants to call any organization for any purpose, SOAR is a great way to make contact and get results.

Summary

SOAR is an unprecedented formula for getting through to a decision maker or someone of high influence 90 percent of every net new dial. (The typical percent for "getting in" on a net new call is 10 to 15 percent.) SOAR represents a compelling shift when it comes to making contact with decision makers.

Key points about SOAR:

- SOAR is a research-based formula for driving net new logos.
- SOAR eliminates the "old way" of prospecting.
- Most selling programs teach what to do once you're in; SOAR instructs you how to get in.
- SOAR is measureable with documented ROI on a corporation's initial investment from 200 to 2,000 percent in 12 weeks.
- SOAR is applicable to any industry, product line, sales experience level, or culture.
- SOAR explodes a salesperson's contact rate when making net new dials.

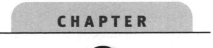

CHAPTER

GETTING READY
TO SOAR

Your Dot

Let's start with what we call your *dot*. This will offer a good start to SOAR execution, and it's what we instruct in all live SOAR corporate programs. Here, we ask you to keep an open mind—executing SOAR requires a shift in your thinking and it may take you out of your comfort zone. But it's important for you to be open to a new way of driving net new business. Imagine a *dot* representing the accumulation of all your knowledge to date. It's the place from which you make all your decisions. Let's take a look at the three stages of what we call your dot.

Stage I: "I know I know."   This is an incredibly dense space filled with your entire belief system. This system was formed by the input from parents, siblings, peers, educators, coaches, bosses, media—anyone you have ever listened to and learned from, and whose words you accepted as truth—along with your experiences. This is the place from which we typically make most of our decisions; it's our own personal way of believing.

Stage II: "I know I don't know."   This represents all the information that you know exists, but don't know much about. (See Figure 2-1.) For example: I know pilots can fly a plane. I also know I don't know how to do this. Surgeons can transplant vital organs. I know it's done, but I don't know how they do it. (Just

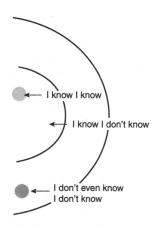

Figure 2-1 *I Know I Don't Know Graph*

think how capable you would be if you had the knowledge in Stage II! Imagine for a moment how your life could change.)

Stage III: "I don't even know I don't know."   Think about all the vast information that is out there that you don't even know you don't know! This segment, "we don't even know we don't know," may be where you find yourself the most challenged when learning about SOAR. Stage III is sometimes called our "blind spot." When you drive you say, "the car next to me was in my blind spot." In other words, you couldn't "see" it. Stage III is similar: we can't always see a possibility if we don't know it exists.

A Closer Look at the Influence of a Person's Dot

In 1982, Drs. Barry Marshall and Robin Warren of Perth, Western Australia, discovered a cure for certain type of ulcer. This new medical discovery was revolutionary. Yet, despite having irrefutable evidence that this new discovery represented a powerful breakthrough in the cure for ulcers, their peers rebutted the evidence. Other doctors couldn't accept this new discovery because they were operating from, "I know what I know." It's a perfect example of how Stage I of the dot can keep us from being open or even able to hear new information because this new information *doesn't align with our prevailing beliefs*. Despite the fact that Dr. Marshall and Dr. Warren's peers were exceptionally talented physicians, they simply were not open to the new remedy because it was outside of their line of thinking. It took 15 years of healing ulcer patients through this new medical breakthrough before Dr. Marshall and Dr. Warren's discovery was finally accepted. Think about that! It took highly educated professionals *15 years* to accept that something outside of their current belief paradigm could be possible, let alone successful!

Being open to *new* ideas that do not match your current way of thinking is vital to your success. New ideas come from new ways of thinking; keeping an open mind in all aspects of your life is essential if you want to grow past where you currently are. The best possible way to harness the power of SOAR is to maintain an open mind: that is, be willing to shift your position—your current beliefs—your dot. Much of what you may learn will come from Stage III, "I don't even know I don't know." As you discover the secrets of SOAR and begin to see the amazing psychology that makes it work, we ask that you *do your best to stay open.* Your current dot will want to judge; it will want to say, "this information isn't right." Being judgmental is a natural state of mind, but if you can stay open to a new way to make contact, you will dramatically increase your results.

The Importance of a Good Call List

After observing thousands upon thousands of live dials with a multitude of salespeople from various industries, we have found one thing they all seem to have in common: they were all working from an ineffective prospecting list.

SOAR instruction culminates with live dialing by the attendees, so all participants are asked to bring a list of at least 10 net new companies they want to contact along with the name of the person they would like to speak to. The list includes the CEO and additional C-level contacts. We request an absolutely "cold" list to prove the power of SOAR. Once the mechanics and mindset of how to reach decision makers is delivered, the SOAR instructor asks for volunteers to dial, live, in front of the class. Most of the time, the dialing process reveals that the call list is inaccurate by approximately 40 percent! Our instructors have found that even top organizations are using error-filled call lists.

We recently trained an organization that told us all new salespeople were given an "excellent" list to call from. They said the lists were "scrubbed" and very accurate. Once we began the live dialing segment of SOAR we discovered that, sure enough, approximately 40 percent of the names on the list were inaccurate. Many of the company executives were in the room when the training was taking place and observed the live dialing segment. They were stunned that the list they thought was scrubbed was, in fact, pretty bad. List companies tout the accuracy of their lists; many claim their lists are consistently upgraded and are 96 percent accurate. But when our Dialexis instructors tested the statement, it turns out not to be the case.

It's unbelievable how bad call lists are—wrong numbers; companies out of business; no one by that name works there; fax lines listed as phone numbers; and so on. Sometimes dialers will have to make three or four attempts in front of the SOAR instructor before they even get a company to answer the phone. What's unfortunate about having inaccurate lists is that it daunts the spirit of those dialing. During the class this isn't fatal because we encourage them to try another call. But just think how demoralizing a bad call list is for salespeople when they are in their own office. There is no one there to say "it's OK, make another call," or, "let's get it this time, its going to happen." When they are in their office, they are on their own. Since most of us don't like prospecting in the first place, an error-filled list is sometimes all it takes to get us off track and ready to throw in the towel or to abandon the call process entirely!

A clean, scrubbed list is a big deal, and finding a solution to delivering accurate prospecting lists to salespeople should be a priority. Sales managers need to pay attention to the damage done to the mindset of a salesperson when an ineffective list is delivered—a list that is 40 percent inaccurate becomes a frustrating factor for salespeople, and that often leads salespeople to discontinue calling. It's even worse when salespeople are expected to find their own list. Newer salespeople either don't seek out their own list, expect the company to provide a scrubbed list, or are unsure of where to find the best list. The top performing sales professionals that we have experienced don't wait to be given a list of prospects; they create a list through research, purchasing, and "scrubbing" their own lists then use a customer relationship management (CRM) system to keep it current. That is their gold mine—and it pays dividends if used and maintained properly.

In reality, if you are working for a company that expects you to drive net new business, it really shouldn't be your responsibility to "scrub" your own prospecting or account list, but as they say, if you want it done right you might just have to do it yourself. Here are some techniques to help you:

1. Ask your marketing department for support.

2. Hire an intern to "scrub" your list by updating the information online.

3. Hire a stay-at-home professional to confirm information by calling the accounts.

4. Begin building a list of referrals from your existing clients or personal business contacts.

5. Lastly, you can refine your list as you make calls yourself.

Determining Your Prospecting Strategy

Generally speaking, it shouldn't be much of a challenge for any salesperson to determine the target company they want to reach out to; after all, you know the product or service you sell, and the company you work for certainly provides direction on who they want to do business with. If you are with a smaller organization, however, you may not have the luxury of the support provided by a Fortune 500 company, so you may have to seek out the targets you want from scratch. If this is the case, then there are two strategies you may want to consider: the first is transactional targets, and the second is larger relationship targets. It's up to you to decide how to strategize your prospecting campaign. Transactional or relationship . . . networking or referrals . . . or maybe social media . . . it's your choice. If you want fast money and you are on full commission, then transactional is a must. However, you still need to develop relationships while you pursue transactional business. Ultimately, your decision will likely be a mix of methodology. If you have an attraction to one over another, protect yourself and consider collaborating with someone who has a different prospecting strategy than you do.

A True Story from a High Commission Sales Career

When we were in commercial real estate, there wasn't much training pertaining to finding business. The pattern most brokers employed was simply to go to the streets and cold call. As a result, we became a product of those who played the brokerage game before us. We didn't have a formal list (most brokers didn't), so we just went to the streets to prospect like the other brokers did—and did it relentlessly. We would be on the streets at 7 a.m. and wrap the prospecting segment of the day at 4:30 p.m., then head back to the office to do paperwork. We even made calls on the street on Saturday. Doing this aggressively for 18 months had positive results. On the plus side, Dave was rookie of the year out of 250 new candidates throughout the United States. He made great money and he was considered an up-and-comer. The bad news is he was really exhausted. After all, he was working six days a week, driving the streets, walking the streets, making follow-up calls, and acclimating to the marketplace. He didn't have lunch with the guys, hang out, or tell jokes. It was strictly a game of survival.

Unbeknownst to Dave, he was becoming a transactional broker. Transitional brokers make a call, get a deal . . . that's it. If they call on a target that isn't quite ready to move to a new building, they move on right away, looking for someone who wants to act "now." At the start of the year, Dave recalled how daunting it was have no business lined up for the coming year. He would meet with other transactional brokers right after New Year's for a cup of coffee and discuss what he was going to do to find deals in the year ahead. It was brutal.

The brokerage company was constantly hiring, and they would seek only the best of candidates. Dave noticed that they were beginning to bring in IBM and Xerox salespeople. During their first years there, these Fortune 500 guys failed to make the top 10. Dave used to say, "These guys are nothing without their IBM card. Now that they are in a street fight game, they can't handle it." Then, after three or so years of meager production, they suddenly started to appear on the top 10 list in rankings . . . then in the top 5 . . . and ultimately, at the top. Every year thereafter they would always be in the top 5 percent or greater. What caused them to stay up at the top? Soon it became clear: they were focused on relationship selling. They were targeting top firms and slowly making progress toward handling the account's real estate. Their strategy was due in part to the training they had received at the big Fortune 500 company: they knew that each relationship account would continue to produce year after year as long as the account was being serviced well. That meant that when January came around and we were trying to figure out how to make money in the coming year, they were relaxed, knowing that the key accounts they controlled would continue to produce transactions for them. Essentially, while most traditional brokers were running at full speed just trying to find a deal quickly, the Xerox and IBM salespeople the company hired had captured big oil wells. It was a lesson we learned that forever changed our approach to selling. Today, we utilize both transactional and relationship development to drive our revenue. As a result, our ability to drive business is significantly more consistent.

How Many New Business Calls a Day Are Right?

We frequently get asked this question by salespeople from all industries. Of course, there is no one answer. Although there are many factors to consider, here are four to get you started.

Leadership's Directives.   Essentially, you are expected to do what your leadership team asks of you. We have one client who wants 100 calls a day from each of his sales professionals! As you can probably guess, making 100 calls a day is strictly a transactional event—no deep conversations, no interaction, just a quick introduction and a closing question. If there is no interest from whoever answers, it's off to another call. Seems crazy, but it works for them. They are a very successful organization (and yes, their salespeople bang out 100 calls a day!).

Maintaining a Territory with Named Accounts. If you are assigned "named accounts," you may be making fewer calls each day since you are focused on the key accounts you are covering. Of course, it depends on how many named accounts you have been assigned. Sometimes the number of calls you are expected to make in a day are face-to-face calls, and sometimes they may require using the telephone. Either way, it's up to management, and if face-to-face is the objective, then you can do the math. Considering drive time, preparation, wait time, and so on, you may only make three to five calls per day.

Salary vs. Straight Commission/Self-Employed. We've observed that when salespeople receive a substantial salary, it often dilutes their interest in making net new dials. If the salary is enough to feed the family and the boss isn't pushing too hard for new business development calls, then that's exactly what happens . . . few or no new calls. On the other hand, if you are on straight commission without a draw, then new business development prospecting is the order of the day. Salespeople who are on straight commission essentially "eat what they kill." If no one is providing food, then we hunt.

In other words, the number of calls per day (or week) may be impacted by your compensation structure, your personal goals, and the pressure exuded from the company. We can say this: consistently sharpen your skills by making the number of net new dials needed to make your goal.

Financially Solvent or Cash-Poor. If you have enough money to keep you going, you may not have the mental mindset to make net new dials. On the other hand, if you are cash-poor, you are likely to be highly motivated to get to the streets or hit the telephone. Fear is a big motivator when it comes to demand generation—very little money with no backup cash presents a real crisis. When you top it off with the responsibility of a family, car payment, house payment, or rent, working relentlessly may be the only option. With this kind of pressure, you are in the field at 7 a.m. and home at 7 p.m. Not having options is a great motivator for getting salespeople moving! Once you adopt this type of relentless work ethic, it establishes a pattern, so going after *new* business becomes a part of your DNA. The number of dials per day may be dictated by this kind of pressure.

Desk Organization and Consistent Prospecting

Being aware of your personal organizational style is important. You may prefer a well-organized desk or be the type of person that collects so much data that, to the outside world, your office looks like a bomb went off. Whatever your organizational style is, it's important that it works for you and that it provides a platform to help you drive net new business. So, how do you organize your desk, laptop, or work area to do this?

Many people are visual, so having current client files physically on their desk helps keep them on track. Some salespeople like everything on their desk to relate to *only* business, so they have a very simple, clean workspace. Other salespeople have *everything* on their desk—dry cleaning hanging on their cube wall, paraphernalia everywhere, and so forth. Again, whatever style works best for you is fine; it's your choice. However, no matter what you do, *have something in your workspace that represents a key motivator* for you so you will consistently be focused on driving net new business. That might be a photo of your wife, husband, girlfriend, kids, new car—anything that's a personal motivator. Pick something that inspires you and drives you to build net new business and get it up in your cube or office and proudly state: "This is what I want, and I am going to get it by the end of the year" (or whatever time frame you declare). Plaster an image of what you want right in your line of vision and start dialing!

A True Story

We know one "rookie" salesperson whose motivator not only worked for her, but connected her with her peers, too. This woman knew that if she hit her sales budget, she would be rewarded with a bonus that would allow her to buy a Harley-Davidson motorcycle. So she posted a two-by-four-foot glossy photograph of this beautiful machine in her cube as her motivator. Being new to the group, she hadn't made many friends yet, but when she plastered this poster of the Harley up in her workspace, many curious salespeople would come over and introduce themselves and ask about the photo. She was always thrilled to tell them about her goal and how she had discovered her love of riding when her husband had purchased a bike, and she now wanted one of her own. Despite the fact that she had no experience in sales (in fact, she was previously a teacher), she got the bonus and got her Harley! She also gained the respect of her peers. Her Harley was her motivator.

The Importance of a CRM

Having the tools that help you make net new business dials is essential to your success. One critical tool is a well-designed CRM. Most organizations are using some kind of CRM to keep track of client information, communications, and contact data. Some CRMs are purposeful and efficient when it comes to prospecting and lead generation (we use Salesforce as our CRM, and it is an incredible tool for tracking new business calls; in fact, some of our clients have adapted their Salesforce CRM to include a SOAR tab to track net new dials). If the CRM you are using helps initialize target calls, then you are likely benefiting from a system that is effective and will support you in making net new dials.

If, on the other hand, you have to search your CRM for a contact list, you may get off-track and ultimately not make many calls. Try keeping a list of potential target accounts on your desk where you can clearly see it. Label it your "target dials" or "leads list." This list should consist of net new organizations that you want to prospect. We have been told by a number of salespeople that having a paper prospect list right next to their telephone was a great daily reminder for them to call and easier to access than having to scroll through their computer. They said they would easily get distracted and into e-mails and other projects without a visual reminder on their desk to help them focus on demand generation.

We recommend you organize yourself to fit your personal style as well as to accommodate your organization's structure. Either way, decide to make driving net new business easier. If you choose the above approach, when you come to the office, you can check your calendar, look over your e-mails, and then jump on your prospecting list, whether it's on your CRM or right next to your telephone. Once you have accomplished the pressing things, log on or reach over to your list and make a few net new dials. Then record the call information in your CRM. Over the period of a day, you can typically make 3 to 10 net new business development dials using this simple organizational suggestion. It's not rocket science; it's just a way for some salespeople to stay the course. If you don't have the list on your CRM or desk in hard copy, we know you can get busy and move from one thing to the next, never making new calls. On the other hand, if the list with the target companies is right there, it's just easier to take action.

Call Measurement

Why measure? Because it allows us to see our progress. That's why the experts suggest taking photos before beginning a diet or exercise program. They want you to see how well you're doing by comparing how you look as you exercise to how you used to look before you started working out. Most salespeople are motivated by results, so it's critical to measure call progress—critical. Knowing how well you did at the end of the day and identifying where you can improve your results becomes a clear success formula. It gives you a road map for developing your contact skills and, subsequently, your overall sales results.

When you use SOAR, consider the following keys to determine how well you are doing on your calls: *gross dials*, *N/A*, *net dials*, *DM*, *HI*, and *appointments* (see Glossary of Terms). Once you make contact, it is your value statement and objection handling that determines the number of appointments that you achieve. So, a low rate of appointments against contacts provides you with the opportunity to sharpen your value statement, value statement delivery, and handling of objections. Without specific measurement, you will find it difficult to diagnose your areas of vulnerability.

Again, the great thing about measuring your dialing is that you get a very clear understanding if you are using SOAR correctly and if your value statement and objection handling are giving you the results you want. Remember, you should get an 80 percent to 90 percent contact rate with decision makers and high influencers. If your total is below 70 percent as a combined number, then you need to look at how you are executing SOAR. We consider anything below a 70 percent combined contact rate to be an inefficient use of SOAR. Given that decision-maker contact generally runs 46 percent and high influencers at 44 percent, you will be able to see from your call tracking if you're in alignment with the SOAR national averages. Knowing this provides you with the ability to reassess if it is your lack of *intention* or an inability to follow the SOAR formula that is the issue. In a way, having a call measurement sheet in front of you is encouraging since you get to see your immediate success. If you prefer to use your CRM and it has a SOAR identifier or field, this is an excellent tool to use to measure your call results. For those of you who may not have a computer-based contact management system, you can use this simple tracking format. (See Figure 2-2.) Either way, measuring calls daily is a worthwhile effort.

Date	Gross dials	N/A	Net dials	DM	HI	MOM	Appt.	Comments
Mon	10	4	6	2	3	0	1	
Tue	4	1	3	1	1	0	0	
Wed	8	3	5	2	2	1	2	
Thur	6	2	4	2	2	0	1	
Fri	8	4	4	0	3	1	1	
Total	36	14	22	7	11	2	5	
%		39%	61%	32%	50%	9%	23%	
Running SOAR stats	100	40%	60%	46%	44%	10%	20%+	

Figure 2-2 *Call Measurement Example*

Summary

There are critical elements a salesperson should have before executing net new dials. Developing a successful demand generation platform involves more than simply picking up the telephone each day and meeting the organization's expectations.

Key points about getting ready to SOAR:

- Have a "scrubbed" list of targets to dial (most lists are inaccurate).
- Successful dialing begins with a *mindset* that connects the assignment of making net new calls with a powerful reason why demand generation matters.
- Determining what to say *before* dialing is paramount.
- Measuring each net new dial reveals areas where the call process can be improved.
- Two key areas of measurement are percent of contacts and percent of appointments.

MINDSET: ITS CONNECTION TO CALL RELUCTANCE AND TOP PERFORMANCE

Definition of Mindset

We are going to speak about mindset throughout this book and the impact it has when it comes to driving net new business. The word *mindset,* as used in the context of this book refers to:

1. A mental inclination, tendency, or habit

2. A fixed state of mind

3. A particular way of thinking: a person's attitude or set of opinions about something

Why Call Reluctance Exists: Seven Surprising Facts That Impact a Salesperson's Mindset

In the course of training a multitude of salespeople across the globe, one of the things we have discovered is a lack of mindset when it comes to achievement, particularly when it comes to prospecting achievement. Generally speaking, we were not surprised to find that salespeople simply don't like to prospect. They know that it's a part of their responsibility; they realize it's directly related to their personal income; and, most of all, they know upper management expects it. Nevertheless, it's generally not a favorite thing to do and can even be viewed as distasteful, particularly if it involves driving net new business without having a warm lead. Here are seven realities we have discovered that impact a salesperson's mindset when it comes to prospecting.

Fact #1: They Aren't Held Accountable

We have trained salespeople with the SOAR process all over the world and can tell you that the primary reason salespeople consistently resist prospecting has to do with accountability. For whatever reason, many sales managers miss the opportunity to measure prospecting effort.

We once read somewhere that "whatever is inspected is respected." Accountability simply makes things happen.

A True Story About Accountability

We introduced SOAR to a very successful high-tech organization in Atlanta, Georgia, with approximately 100 sales reps and three key sales leaders. The CEO elected to bring the SOAR program into the organization and wanted measurement to validate that their investment with the program was worthwhile. As a result, we recommended a three-day program, which included one day with the managers and two days with the sales team. Prior to training the sales team, we spent an intense day with the managers, outlining what their salespeople were about to experience and how we would be measuring results. We explained the various excuses they could expect from their team following the training (based upon our experience with other companies).

By the end of the first day, the managers stated they were fully committed to "stay the course" for the 90-day tracking period, keep the reps on target to a certain number of net new dials per day, and record all call progress and details. As we mentioned, the program was to be measured over a 90-day period, which included measuring the number of dials, contacts with decision makers, high influencers, appointments, pipeline, closed revenue, goal as a percentage, and a few other metrics the company requested. All net new dials were validated to be SOAR-driven on their CRM.

As part of the measurement process, six conference calls were scheduled over the 90-day tracking period between Dialexis and the management team after program completion. A Dialexis SOAR instructor and coach were assigned to the task. During each of the post scheduled calls, managers would report progress for their team and receive coaching from Dialexis. (The CEO chose not to be a part of the six calls; he left it to his sales managers.)

Prior to each call, the managers were required to send Dialexis their team's measurement numbers so we would be able to have meaningful discussions on the telephone and coach accordingly. After two of the scheduled calls, the managers began to crumble. The data began arriving late, some of the managers did not show up for the scheduled calls or were late, and oftentimes the numbers they were reporting were mathematically incorrect. In the end, the program with SOAR died. The original investment was lost by the client, and the frustration Dialexis experienced was substantial since our reputation was on the line as well.

We contacted the CEO and explained. He apologized for sloppy performance by his team and said, "Let's do it again—but right this time." The company reengaged with Dialexis once again and paid another fee. We arrived in Atlanta to meet with the original management team.

Guess how the story ends? The same thing happened! The team exhibited a total lack of accountability and responsibility. A few years later, the company went out of business. Prior to the collapse of the second attempt to deliver an effective SOAR program, the CEO called Dialexis to once again apologize for his management team's lack of accountability and performance. This failure represented one of two SOAR failures out of hundreds of organizations who experienced SOAR successfully over the years. When we review the percentage of companies and leaders that stand strong in the area of accountability, we discovered that the vast majority don't hold their salespeople accountable.

The bottom line is, frequently sales managers simply don't stay the course. Sometimes this is due to their workload, and sometimes it's because top leadership isn't holding *them* accountable. The organizations that stay the course with SOAR make between 200 percent and 2,000 percent in 12 weeks on their initial investment! All it takes is commitment to the process.

Fact #2: They Don't Know How to Prospect

As we mentioned in Chapter 1, many sales managers believe that prospecting on the telephone is "dead" or ineffective. As a result, salespeople are not being trained effectively. They generally conduct telephone prospecting using the old BTN + L way, a method that is highly discouraging. Think about it: if a salesperson makes 100 calls and contacts only 5 or 10 decision makers . . . that's pretty discouraging. Then, when they present their value statement upon making contact and they only achieve an appointment 10 or 20 percent of the time, that allows for a conclusion that calling cold on the telephone just isn't the way to go. Although prospecting cold isn't the only way to drive net new business, it is in fact still a very successful way, if done correctly.

Fact #3: They Believe It's for Rookies

When salespeople are new to selling, we refer to them as "rookies." Rookies generally do whatever it takes to win. They tend to have cooperative attitudes and do what they are told to do because they want to be successful, and one of the things they do is prospect relentlessly without resistance. As salespeople gain experience, they ultimately capture key accounts. Now the money pours in, and since they are doing well, they stop prospecting. Demand generation takes a backseat since most of their efforts are focused on the key accounts they already have. When they are encouraged to continue prospecting for net new business, they often say, "that's for rookies" (and if they don't say it, they think it). Now that they are among the senior ranks, it seems beneath them to have to prospect on the telephone again. Unfortunately, as we all know, all oil wells dry up. Unless salespeople are consistently prospecting, they are at risk for loss of accounts. They don't have to use the telephone as the only means for finding new accounts; it's just that it happens to be an effective way to discover new business if done with a proven formula. Despite the fact that we at Dialexis have been selling for over 30 years, we continue to prospect. Yes, we network and use referrals, but we still use the telephone to contact new target accounts. We no longer sit at our desk and bang out call after call; rather, we are strategically using the SOAR process ourselves to contact net new logos. (We define *new logos* as companies you don't already sell to.) We may only make one or two new net dials per day, but we still use the telephone as a lead generating strategy.

Fact #4: Their Base Salary Is Too High

A coyote hunts because it has to. A domestic animal doesn't because it doesn't have to. If you pay enough base salary, your reps may not feel the pain to hunt; they may become "domesticated." It is human nature to seek the easy way. One example of an "easy way out" is a big salary. Give people enough food to eat and they won't be hungry. We all seek the easy way; few, if any, want to do what they dislike to do if they can find a way out. This is even true for us. We hate doing hard stuff like prospecting, and if we didn't have to, we wouldn't! Certainly, there are salespeople who would look at a large base salary and say to themselves, "This is a great start. By adding net new prospecting on top of this salary I can really make some big money!" But most people don't think this way. So, look at your compensation plan. Again, we're not saying that a high base salary prevents all salespeople from prospecting, but, on the whole, a large salary can crush motivation for picking up the phone and making a net new dial. Salespeople may say they will do the calling, but watch closely and you may find the words don't match their actions. A big salary often leads to call reluctance.

Fact #5: It's Too Hard

Most people avoid difficult tasks. Salespeople are no different when it comes to prospecting. Being faced with a sales manager that believes that making tons of calls is the way to prospect creates a formidable blockade to a salesperson's mindset. As we said, prospecting by the numbers is just plain crazy; it creates attrition, resistance, and resentment. Net new prospecting for the most part can be a tough challenge, and not providing a powerful solution only creates more resistance; it simply becomes too hard in the mind of the salesperson. So, shifting the way salespeople contact can provide a big difference in their mindset. Adopting a SOAR approach does not guarantee that salespeople will suddenly love cold calling, but it will at least give them the opportunity to shift to a positive mindset since they will discover that they now have a fighting chance to make contact with decision makers.

Fact #6: The Company Culture Doesn't Demand It

We know this is the case based upon our experience in the field with clients. Some organizations within the commercial real estate, office equipment, telecommunications, and other industries usually make it their culture. Most companies, however, only talk about it. The expectation for new business development just never takes priority in many organizations; as a result, net new prospecting doesn't happen. Why would a salesperson develop a prospecting mindset if the company doesn't have one?

Fact #7: They Are in the Top Ranking and Think They Will Stay There

Salespeople can get arrogant quickly and stop prospecting even faster if you give them a few plaques that say they are Number One. I don't know if they are to blame; it's really more about how they are led and what the expectations of them are. Most "big-shot salespeople" were allowed to get that way. Once salespeople break through to the top 20 percent or higher, they often drop the one thing that may have been the greatest contributor to their rise: prospecting to drive net new logos. It's easy to do, since prospecting is a dreaded event anyway in most mindsets. Give salespeople a few big accounts, a big salary, look the other way, don't hold them accountable, award them with titles and plaques—and watch prospecting take a nose dive. Salespeople get to a top rank status and think it will never end. The mindset that originally took them to the top suddenly shifts. They now feel they have arrived and actually believe they will always stay at the top. If you are a sales rep, just remember: all oil wells dry up.

The Secret to a Powerful Mindset: Discovering Your Magnet

We'll use the word *magnet* to stand for a dream, goal, vision, and so on. When we speak of something you really want, we will refer to it as your *magnet*. We believe that *pain* and *fear* tend to *push* a person while a *dream* or *vision* tends to *pull*—just like a magnet. (See Figure 3-1.)

We hear it all the time: salespeople frequently *say* that they want to be the best and they want to be in the top performing group within the organization. But no matter how many salespeople *say* they intend to be at the top, few make it. Have you ever wondered why only a certain number of salespeople actually make it to the top percentile within a sales organization? Of course, we categorize the ones who make it as the top 20 percent. Our view is, if salespeople have enough pain/fear, such as the thought that they may lose their job if they don't perform well, they will be motivated to perform; or, if they have little savings and the salary isn't enough to support their family, they will also be motivated by pain/fear. On the opposite end of

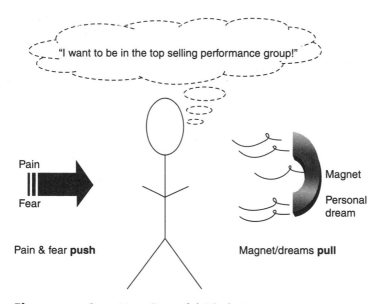

Figure 3-1 *Secret to a Powerful Mindset*

the spectrum, if they have a compelling magnet, something that *pulls* them into action such as discovering their personal vision or dream, they will be *pulled* by that vision. Sometimes both exist and you will see exceptional commitment to performance. The problem is, most salespeople are given substantial salaries and great benefits, so the pain/fear factor may be greatly diminished. The other discovery we have found is that many salespeople don't have a compelling vision! At least, they haven't discovered their vision. As a result, since there is little or no pain/fear *pushing them* and there is no compelling or clear vision/magnet *pulling them*, the result is that nothing happens. It doesn't really matter what they *say* they intend to do; it's not going to happen.

Ask yourself, what is the motivator if it isn't pain/fear or vision/magnet? Salespeople *say* they are going to hit their quota all the time; they say they are going to aggressively drive net new business. We know they aren't lying and they really mean it when they say it, but in the end it doesn't happen. What would cause a salesperson to reach the top if there isn't some kind of motivator? We don't want to have to motivate through fear, and we don't want salespeople to have a crisis in their life, so the only other possibility is to help them discover their vision/magnet.

As we said, we have found over the many years that most salespeople we meet don't seem to be able to define a vision. When we ask them what they really want, they can't come up with much more than something like, "I want to be financially stable," or, "I want to have a good life," or, "I want a better house," or, "I don't really know." When we ask for more detail, they rarely know the answer. As a result, when it comes to their careers, most are just rambling along. They have no real purpose other than to work hard, do their best, and just see what comes their way. Ultimately, many become negative because the pressure is not offset by a dream. On the other hand, we find most people can handle pressure and do the most difficult of tasks *if they feel they are on the way to fulfilling their dream*. Without the dream (magnet), they easily lose focus over time. So when it comes to *net new prospecting* (which, as we have said, most salespeople dread), they may diligently prospect in the beginning, but ultimately burn out or excuse out because they just simply hate making a net new cold call. The only hope of getting salespeople to do what they inherently dislike is to apply consequence, which generates fear, or help them find their magnet. If they say that money is their magnet, the important question to ask is "why?"—The answer may lead to their true magnet.

Let's say your vision is represented by Figure 3-2 below—your magnet, as we said. If a salesperson loses focus, he may find himself becoming negative or underperforming. If a salesperson has a powerful magnet, he rarely loses focus.

Figure 3-2 *Life's Distractions*

When you see salespeople who perform well and you think to yourself, "why can't I do that?" the answer is most likely that they are operating with a compelling magnet in their life. From our experience, it's the true secret to a powerful mindset. Find your magnet; shift your results!

We are often asked, "how can I discover my magnet, because I don't want to wait for pain to be my motivator?" or "I just don't know what I really want, how do you recommend I find out?" Here is what we suggest: go to the beach!

Easy Steps to a Mindset Shift: Go to the Beach

You heard it right: go to the beach. We live by the beach, so it's the place we often go to when we need to reset our vision or magnet. So, we coined the phrase "go to the beach" to mean going to a place to get centered, find your vision, and reconnect with what's important to you. Your beach might be a park, a lake, your den, or wherever you feel you can "deep think." It's simply a place to determine what motivates you and what you are passionate about.

If you are a morning person, go early in the morning, because that's probably when you are most alert and focused. Find an isolated spot where there are no people to distract you. If you find you think better at night, then find a quiet place where you feel you can gather your thoughts uninterupted. Going to the beach is about tapping into *what inspires you.* Once you find what inspires you (your magnet), you then have a powerful motivation to do whatever it takes to get you to your magnet, including, but not limited to, driving net new business. If you believe prospecting will help you get to your magnet, you're on your way. Your beach trip is *not* a strategy session about the new accounts you will be calling on. This is about what's fundamentally important to you. It is about finding your passion, vision, and internal drive—the inspiration that moves you. A note: discovering what matters most to you doesn't mean you should quit your job; it means you have found a motivator that makes prospecting effortless, because finding net new business can ultimately give you what you *really* want. Knowing what you want is a powerful incentive.

Here are a few practical suggestions for going to the beach. If you are currently working, go on a weekend, take a writing pad, find a quiet spot, and dig into your thoughts. (You may be gone for one hour or five hours; whatever it takes. You will know when you are done because you'll just *feel finished.*) When you are at your beach, start by asking yourself questions like, "what's important to me?" "where do I want to be in the next 5 years? 10 years?" Just dig around in your thoughts, writing stuff down until you complete an intellectual and emotional "dump." Ask yourself not only what is important and why it matters, but when you want to achieve it. Ask yourself if you are willing to pay the price. Write until your hand hurts and you are emotionally complete. *That's* a beach trip! This will help you discover your dream.

Remember this, however, one trip to the beach may not be enough to discover your motivator, your magnet. It may take several times; it may take months or years until something really hits you, but start the process. When you do, your subconscious begins to work for you. The key is to get out of your head and into your heart. Do your best to discover what your true passion is. Let yourself open up and think big thoughts. We've had so many people tell us how they had a breakthrough when they thought they were at a blocking point. Just when they thought they were stuck, suddenly, something opened up on their beach trip.

Keep digging until you find what is most important to you (and your family or loved ones), and why. Not what you think you *should* be doing, but what really is important to you; something that excites and energizes you. That's what you are looking for, and this will be your greatest piece of the puzzle for outrageous success. You will end up with a powerful purpose and the driver for all your endeavors. If that means insane focus on prospecting, then finding net new business or learning to prospect consistently will no longer seem like a burden. Instead, it will be an exciting adventure to prospect for new business because you are on your way to something that the results of prospecting will ultimately deliver.

A True Story About Discovering Your Passion

Several years ago, we introduced a group of salespeople to the concept of going to the beach. Everyone went individually and, the next month, we got together to discuss our experiences. We heard many interesting stories, but one person in particuliar stood out. He said he had uncovered a dilemma at the beach. He explained that he had realized he really wanted to become a pastor and start a church! Now, this was a guy that was selling furniture! Most everyone was caught off guard, but we really got behind him and asked, "so what's the dilemma?" He explained that the company he was with didn't seem to

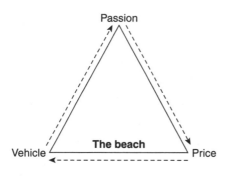

Figure 3-3 *The Beach*

be the vehicle that could take him to his passion. We asked the group to share their thoughts; did they think selling furniture supported him in reaching his goal, in any way? Everyone wanted to support this guy and did their best to determine how selling furniture could help him get there. In minutes, the answer came to them. Everyone agreed that he was going to need money to start a church. They all determined that working in sales at his organization could support him in getting seed money to start his church. The guy agreed—his company was the vehicle to lead him to his passion. (See Figure 3-3.)

The moral of the story is to be open to the possibility that your sales career and the organization that you are working for can support you in getting to your passion. Find your dream and start driving net new business.

Remember, your beach trip is a place where you look for the thing that is really most important to you. It doesn't have to be "save the whales" or "eliminate poverty." It may be as simple as helping someone you love go to college, buy a new car, or to take a special trip. The key is to find what truly motivates you and what deeply inspires you. When you find it—your magnet—it will become all you can think about. Once you have your magnet, you will no longer be daunted by prospecting, going the extra mile, or any other blockade to your success. You won't have time for negativity, for complaining about the company or your circumstances. Driving net new business will no longer represent a blockade for you. You will only be consumed by your magnet.

Tip: if you are married or in a comitted relationship, we recommend you both go to the beach, but separately. Agree to meet later, in one hour or five hours; take as long as each of you needs for your beach trip. Upon reconnecting, you can share your beach discoveries and see if you are both on track relative to your declarations. You might be surprised to learn you were emotionally heading for a disconnect, or perhaps you will discover that you both want the same thing. So, if you are not sure what you want, make an appointment with yourself to go to your beach and start the digging.

Here is a great quote from a business coach named John Cundif out of Colorado. (If you want to meet John, contact us and we will be happy to personally introduce you.) He really helped us to discover our own magnet. See if you can understand the meaning of what we got from John. John said, "A successful project begins with your passion, and then you find the way. With an unsuccessful project, you look for the way, believing it will reveal your passion." Essentially what the quote says is that a successful project begins with your "passion," and then the "way" will be revealed!

Incidently, if you discover your magnet is *not* working for the company you are with, your endeavors in the company may be ultimately linked to delivering you to your passion.

A True Story About Losing Focus

A few years ago, we supported a young man during the rise of his selling career. He was very talented and exceptionally driven. Our contact with one another was limited to a few times a year, but it was consistant and we were impressed with how well he was progressing up the corporate ladder. After a few years of successful selling, we learned that he had accepted a leadership role and was managing a group of salespeople. About six months after he accepted this new job, we reached out to congratulate him on his success, and much to our surprise, we found him to be in a very negative place. He told us how his company was a mess, how the top management "didn't get it," and how frustrated he was. We were surprised to hear him speak this way, since he was always a very positive guy, super motivated, and considered a sales star. So what happened? We had a feeling that when he expressed how disfunctional the company was and how management didn't get it, that he thought we would sympathize with him and support his negative perspectives. Instead, we simply said, "it sounds as though you have lost your vision." He asked us what we meant. We replied, "if you were committed to a powerful vision you wouldn't have time to be negative." This stopped him in his tracks. He replied, "I think you're right, maybe I need to take another look at what I stand for and what my magnet is."

When any individual is moving toward a powerful vision or being pulled by a strong magnet, it's impossible to have time to be negative. Michael Jordan of the Chicago Bulls described a playoff game as being "between me and the basket; the defender has nothing to do with it." That hit us like a bolt of lightening. What he was saying is that distractions are irrelevant. It doesn't matter what is happening outside you; when a vision is powerful, there are no distractions!

So, if you are losing motivation, or you're not getting the results you want in your life or your selling career—or you are just simply slipping into negativity—check your magnet. It may be time to get back to the basics and go to the beach. Your deep passion is extremely powerful, so be sure you've tapped into it. Even if you've gone to the beach or think you know what you're creating, keep it fresh and alive by going back at least once a year so you can stay on course, or, if you discover your vision has shifted, plot a new path.

Mindset vs. Tactics

When it comes to exceptional performance, do you think the advantage would go to mindset or tactics? In the case of sales production, the 80/20 rule states that 80 percent of the business is achieved by

20 percent of the salespeople. If we were to ask you where you want to be in sales results, we're betting you'll say in the top 20 percent or greater. The question is, since all salespeople say they want to be in the top 20 percent, why do some get there while others just talk about it? Why is it that the top salespeople in any organization are at the top?

Take a look at the 10 choices listed below and check which you think is the number one reason top salespeople consistently achieve amazing results in the world of sales:

1. Luck

2. Connections

3. Education

4. Timing

5. Mindset

6. Better territory

7. Tactics

8. Experience

9. Favoritism

10. Innate ability

After decades of selling, leading salespeople, observing top talent, and training all levels of salespeople in a multitude of countries, industries, and organizations, we've found that mindset is what provides the primary advantage when it comes to top sales performance. This is not to say that all the other factors listed are not big contributors, because they are, but when it comes down to the absolute base level of why a salesperson consistently becomes a top achiever, we believe it is because of mindset.

Henry Ford once said, "whether you think you can or whether you think you can't—you're right." Napoleon Hill wrote about the importance of a positive mental attitude in *Think and Grow Rich*, as did Dr. Norman Vincent Peale in his book *The Power of Positive Thinking*. This is a time old philosophy: if you think you can or you think you can't, either way you are right.

So, why is the question "mindset or tactics" so important? We have found that most salespeople believe it's tactics. Salespeople seem to be focused on product knowledge to get what they want. When we conduct live SOAR trainings, less experienced salespeople always gravitate toward the mechanics of SOAR. Nevertheless, we always begin instructing SOAR with mindset, then move into mechanics. Once we begin the mechanics portion of the instruction, the how-to segment of SOAR, we often hear salespeople say, "I liked it when we got to the meat of the training." Most rookie salespeople simply fail to understand how mindset drives results (senior salespeople, however, respond in the opposite fashion).

As you read this book, you will find the answer to reaching decision makers or the C-level executive suite is a blend of mechanics (tactics), psychology, and, of course, mindset. They all work together, but we are certain that mindset is the secret, the real fuel to making things happen. This is the primary reason we coupled mindset with the mechanics of SOAR; we knew the combination was the key to achievement when it comes to making contact with decision makers.

Once you have a mindset of "can do" or "will do" and then add the mechanics of SOAR to your bag, the next step is deciding to go for it. Ask yourself, do you want to be in the top 20 percent in your selling career, or not? Knowing your own personal magnet is the secret to your results.

Performing in the Top 20 Percent

Take a look at Figure 3-4 below and use it to determine if reaching the top 20 percent in your career with your company is worth the effort to get there or if playing in the 80 percent is a better deal for you.

Being in the 80% is considered easy	Getting to the top 20%+ is considered hard
You just have to show up	Dedicated work ethic: long hours Paperwork: reports Travel Relentless prospecting Quota pressure Accountability Responsibilities Meetings
The payoff	**The payoff**
Less money Negative recognition Embarrassment Apartment Local travel: motel Limited ability to invest Limited ability to help others financially Less security Limited medical coverage Limited choices	More money Positive recognition Pride Home Exciting travel: Ritz-Carlton Investments Help others Increased security Best medical coverage More choices

Figure 3-4 *The Price You Pay for Choosing to Play at the 80 Percent or Top 20 Percent+ (What It Takes and Why It's Considered Easy or Hard)*

When you look at the comparison above, you can see that the 80 percent is definitely easier to attain from a work perspective and reaching the top 20 percent is clearly more difficult. The real question is: is the 80 percent *really* easier? It takes very little effort to get there, but the price you pay may be more than you are willing to pay. Essentially, little effort equals little return. So, if you don't like driving new business through calling cold or prospecting in general and all the other things you are required to do to make it to the top 20 percent, you can simply compare that difficulty factor against the difficulty of what you get by being in the 80 percent. With top 20 percent performance, you have to work smart and really pay with effort, but you get a lot in return. With the 80 percent you don't have to do much, but the price you pay in the 80 percent is a reduced lifestyle—perhaps even job loss. So is the goal of being in the top 20 percent worth it? This is still your call, your choice. Once again, you can look at the comparison above and decide if living in the 80 percent is acceptable or doing what is necessary to get to the top 20 percent is worth it. It's your choice. If you choose to play in the top 20 percent, then you should never have complaints about finding net new business in any manner, even cold calling! When you think about it, no one is making you do anything . . . you get to choose.

Being in the top 20 percent does not just mean money—it also means quality of life. Money provides freedom of choice and the ability to do so many things, from sending your kids to a better school or helping your family or contributing to a charity you believe in. You will have freedom of choice; you can choose to experience success on your terms. Being in the top 20 percent is also a source of pride. You will be recognized for your achievements and you will have the ability to share your knowledge and experience with others.

We were training at a national firm a few months ago and there were photos of senior salespeople on the wall. They were identified as Wolf Leaders. These were the top salespeople that were also mentors to the junior salespeople coming up the ranks. During the training, we met a few of these Wolf Leaders because they actually came to the training to pick up new information so they could support the younger salespeople. They commented on how valuable it was to be able to share what they had learned and how it inspired them to achieve at an even greater level. Think about it: when top performers attend a rookie training and are open to be part of the training, it's easy to understand why they are the best.

The Power of Your Story and How It Impacts Mindset

This is another place where you may be challenged to "get off your dot." We began this chapter with a discussion about the importance of finding your passion by going to the beach. Then, we talked about your mindset and how it impacts your sales mental attitude. But there's more. When it comes to high-performance selling, there is an even more powerful force that has a direct impact on your sales perfomance. It's called your "story."

Who you've become may not be who you *really are*. This is the case because who you have become and how you have developed is a case of how other factors influenced you. Since birth, you have been influenced. You didn't just get your parent's genes; you got their belief system or, as we call it, their story. You have been bombarded by years of messaging from powerful outside sources as well as the beliefs of your family. These messages have shaped and reshaped your mindset. Your parents and teachers; your experiences; the media; the community you were raised in; and so on, all had an influence on you.

You can imagine how many kinds of stories we may have created that do not serve us well. How many of us have said, "I want washboard abs," or, "I want a new car," or, "I want to move into a better place and go back to school." If you find you aren't achieving these goals, you will know it's because of your unconscious beliefs, some story you are playing in your mind. Your *story* was most likely formed a long time ago and you are unconsciously proving yourself "right" about that belief, over and over again. For example, if you were a chubby little kid and people made fun of you, you may have made up the story, "I will never be fit or athletic . . . I won't even try because I don't have the body for it." You have the opportunity to dig out old stories that don't serve you or are in your way and replace them with new stories or beliefs, ones that will deliver the results you say you want.

Our dot is already colored in. We just need to be aware of how our story impacts our ability to reach the top 20 percent because it's involved—big time. Our experiences create beliefs and our beliefs create patterns. It can be something as simple as not making a prospecting call because you may have created a story about not wanting to bother someone, or you may have a story that taking risks is not a good thing because it never works out. Whatever you view as "reality," you will move forward in the world to prove it's true by creating evidence you are right about your existing story—your reality. To paraphrase Henry Ford again, if you think you can or think you can't, either way you are right. We attract into our lives the results that we believe to be true. So, if you feel the economy is hindering your sales, then you will seek evidence to prove you are right by having your deals not close, because that solidifies your story. Despite the fact that you have great tactics and a compelling vision, the whole thing can be a disaster if you have a negative hidden story that is unconscious to you. Notice we said *hidden*. That means there are some beliefs that you may not realize are affecting your results. They are buried deep in your subconscious. It is not the fault of the economy, your boss, your spouse, or your fellow salespeople. More than likely, it's the belief or the story that has long been the director in your life. As in a play, the "director" of your results has been your underlying story, which ultimately manifests the results you are getting in your sales career. Despite how hard you try and how strong your convictions are, no matter what you claim you want . . . if under it all is a hidden belief or story that you can't win, then you won't.

The good news is, once you discover what *stories* are in the way of your results, you will see a completely different outcome. Matching a powerful supportive story with competent tactics and a compelling vision yields amazing sales success. You can shift your results if you are aware of your stories and your patterns and their origins. Obtaining what you say you want and dramatically impacting your mindset is possible—if you are willing to look at your results. Mindset combined with mechanics represent the most powerful segments of SOAR. It's how we *think* that makes the most difference in our sales career. Mindset is the key to driving net new business.

Gabriel Nossovitch is the founder and partner of several personal transformation organizations throughout Mexico and Latin America, and he partners with Dialexis in the United States. Many years ago, one of his transformation trainings had a profound impact on our understanding of mindset and its power over our results. We already knew that mindset played a big part in achievement. But one of the things we learned was that when something happens, it really has no meaning at the time of the happening or event; it only takes on meaning *when we decide what the event means to us.* So, something happens that in and of itself is a neutral event; we then apply an interpretation to the event (our "story") and we move forward in our life seeking evidence to prove that our "story" is true. (See Figure 3-5.) The big "aha" was that stories aren't true or false, good or bad, right or wrong . . . they are just stories. We get to choose what we believe. When it comes to cold prospecting or those ugly words, "cold calling," you get to determine if you have a story that doesn't support you. If you have great tactics and a compelling vision, you are off to a strong start. But if success is still not showing up for you, then we can only suggest that there has to be a something underneath, something in your subconscious that is a belief or, as we call it, a story you are manifesting. By looking at your sales results, you get closer to finding your subconscious story. If you are in the top performance in your sales rankings, then we know you must hold a story that you are a strong achiever. Simply look at your sales performance and you will find what story you are holding to be true. Keep stories that serve you, like, "I always find new business," or "I'm good at prospecting," or, "I always hit my sales quota," and so on. Maintain and expand on those powerful stories that drive exceptional results for you in your sales career.

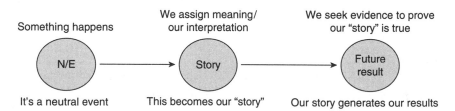

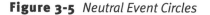

Figure 3-5 *Neutral Event Circles*

A True Story About Shifting Your Mindset

We know a successful salesperson who started his own business and eventually grew his profits to eight million in sales. Over the years he worked like a dog, spending little time with his family and doing all in his power to get his business past the eight million dollar mark—to no avail. When he told us how this frustrating it was, we suggested he attend the Dialexis course EIL (Excellence in Leadership). During the program, he discovered various places where he was holding unconscious beliefs about not wanting partners in his business and other limiting stories that were holding his business back. Following the EIL program, he "shifted" his mindset and dropped the stories that were not supporting him and created new beliefs that empowered his life. It's been five years now and his firm has been on the cover of several magazines, recognized as one of the fastest growing companies in his industry. He has grown by well over 550 percent from his original revenue and continues to experience substantial revenue gain, year after year. More important, he is now taking time for his family. The results he created in his business are possible for you in your selling or managing career, too.

How Your Story Influences Cold Prospecting

Most of us can agree that when we are asked to prospect cold accounts, something within us automatically wants to avoid the task. The mere thought of making a cold call sets off an alarm: "I hate prospecting or calling cold!" If someone's asked to "drive net new business" it's not so bad; it doesn't always set off a negative story. The very words "cold call," however, ring every alarm in a salesperson's mind! This is because they have a story about cold calling, picked up from other salespeople or even sales managers, and it's typically a negative one. Somewhere along the line in a selling career, salespeople are reminded that prospecting is hard. They are told that any process that involves demand generation is tough. Stories like, "don't call on a Monday or Friday" are familiar in most sales organizations, because there is a belief that calling on a Monday or Friday is a bad day because executives are busy. The ranks of any sales organization provide a nest of negative stories about prospecting for net new business.

A True Story About How Shifting Beliefs Shifts Results

We once had a salesperson in our office who didn't think she could sell, let alone make a prospecting call. She was stuck with her story, "I don't think I can sell, I don't like it." She would say, "I'm just not good at it," or "I don't know why, but I just don't like to sell." We asked her if she liked people, and she said, "Absolutely!" We then suggested that she call new prospects and simply *tell* them what she had to offer. We told her, don't *sell* them, just *tell* them why you are calling." She said, "I can do that!" She went on to become our number one salesperson. It was her story that had held her back. She simply changed the word "sell" to "tell" and her results shifted. Consider changing your story and watch your results take off!

A Personal Story

After my parents divorced, my mother took my brother, sister, and me to Chicago, where her stepfather lived and owned a bar on the south side. My mother's stepfather offered her a job running the bar, and he said she could live at the back of the bar where there were a couple of rooms for all of us. I was seven years old at the time, and I didn't think much of it. It was just a new place to live, and although it was noisy at night, I just called it home. I didn't realize that I would eventually make up a story about what it meant to live in the bar: that my mother's life was hard and that it was my dad's fault. I created a deep resentment.

Many years later, I was in Chicago with my wife when I suggested we go look for the bar. We headed to the south side of the city and ultimately found the bar. We went inside, and as soon as we opened the door, the smell of alcohol brought back memories. We sat and talked to the owner, and I explained that I used to live in the bar as a kid. After a while we left, and as we walked out the door and stood on the sidewalk, my wife said to me, "Aren't you glad you came?" I replied, "Absolutely! Because now you can see why I have a chip on my shoulder. Nobody should have to live in a bar." You know what I wanted her to say, right? I wanted her to say, "You poor baby, that must have been so hard for you and your family. Now I understand you so much better!" Well, that isn't what she said. Instead, she replied, "Wow, Dave, were you ever lucky. Look at how fortunate you were to have had that experience. Don't you realize that the bar is where you got your power? It's where your strength and your mindset were born!" I was stunned. She didn't see things as I did; she didn't think I had had a disadvantage. She saw my experience as a positive, amazing event. At that very moment, right on the sidewalk in front of the bar, I *changed my story*. I made up a new story: that I was lucky and that the bar was in fact the best thing that ever happened to me. My new story has served me well. I no longer blame, I don't have it wired that it was anyone's fault. My entire perspective has changed.

Why You May Not Shift Your Story: Payoffs

Sometimes we don't shift our story because of payoffs. What are the payoffs, you ask? We may not be aware of it, but there can be hidden benefits to staying stuck. Consider these: if you complain about prospecting, you may be able to recruit others to feel sorry for you; or you may be able to get attention or avoid responsibility; or you may get to be "right" about your story that cold prospecting doesn't work. Why else would you stay stuck and not drive net new buisiness diligently and consistently if you know, deep down, it will build your success? You may be getting a payoff by staying stuck to your story.

Taking 100 Percent Responsibility for Your Results

One of the paths to a strong and effective mindset when it comes to driving net new business or any part of a sales career is to take 100 percent responsibility for all results. This can be difficult for saleseople, particularly when it comes to demand generation, finding new business, or meeting their quota. Here's why: when salespeople don't succeed at driving net new business, especially when they are making hundreds of new calls and fighting through a bunch of "no's," they often shift blame. After all, if they are trying to make contact with decision makers and doing their best to get appointments with little success, they feel it can't be their fault. They tend to blame the receptionist, the gatekeepers, the decision maker, or C-level executives that may have turned them down. They may even blame their company for not having the best products, or the marketing department because they don't "get" the sales business. Salespeople become the last ones on the list to take responsibility for poor results.

When we train salespeople in the SOAR formula, we often begin the program by asking this question: "What do you want to know about prospecting?" Their answers always seem to be centered around understanding why the receptionist is "out to get them," or lying to them, or why they are intentionally being blocked. We never hear, "I don't know how to succeed," "I don't have the skills," or "I take responsibility for not figuring out the answers." Many salespeople have a mindset that the power to create results is in the hands of someone else, like the receptionist. Consider this question: "How would your strategy shift if you were to take 100 percent responsibility for your results?" This doesn't mean that you are to blame or that it's your fault or you're doing something "wrong"; rather, taking personal responsibility for all your results is simply a vehicle to take a closer look at your behavior and performance. Consider asking yourself, "Why are my attempts at finding net new business subpar? How am I creating results that don't satisfy me or my company?" You will be amazed at the answers that are revealed when you think from a space of 100 percent responsibility. It's a powerful exercise.

If you answer by saying, "But it's not my responsibility," then there isn't much we can do for you. Until you are open to look at all your selling results from a position of "How am I creating my results?" there isn't much *anyone* can do. It's vital that you understand that the power to shift your results in sales or in any part of your life is up to you. When you become humble and vunerable to the extent that you are willing to look solely at yourself for being 100 percent responsible for all the results you get in life, including the results in your sales career, new answers will be revealed.

Learning to take responsibility for everything that occurs in your sales career is challenging. Let's take a look at an example: Let's say you lost an account because the client decided to buy from his brother who is a salesperson with another firm. First, remember that taking 100 percent responsibility doesn't mean you are wrong or that it's your fault. This isn't about blame or shame. Start with viewing this from a space of *your results are just your results*. Now, back up and look at this as if you were taking 100 percent responsibility. Maybe you didn't do all that you could have done with the account you lost. Perhaps you didn't reply to an e-mail promptly, or maybe you didn't make a connection with the decision maker. Ask yourself if you failed to answer a key question correctly or prove yourself to be a trusted advisor . . . and the list goes on. You may have created an opening for the decision maker's brother without even realizing it.

You could also start by talking with your direct report about the loss of the account. Ask your sales manager to shed some light on where you may have gone wrong. The boss may be able to see your blind side; that is, the stuff you can't see. This is where humility is key. But be assured that once you embrace the concept of 100 percent responsibility, powerful opportunities can open up for you. Think about it: *not* adopting the viewpoint that you are the generator of everything in your life only leads to you becoming a victim. Salespeople who are victims rarely exceed expectations. When you begin to realize the power of taking responsibility for all your results—not having any back doors, no excuses, no blaming (including yourself) and that you are truly in charge of calling the shots, your selling results and your personal life will leap forward.

The Power of Negative People and How They Impact Your Mindset

There's a saying that a single negative person can influence 10 positive people. You'd think it would be the other way around, that 10 positive people would be able to influence one negative person, but the power of negativity is strong and compelling. In fact, many of us gravitate toward negative individuals without realizing why, and we often fail to notice the influence they have on our lives. It happens in the office, during sales meetings, or just walking into a presentation; it happens in the field, behind closed doors, or out in the open. Negativity seems to be everywhere. You might think that an organization has hundreds of negative people within its ranks, but not so; it's generally just a few individuals within the company, engaging in gossip and negative talk, who create a negative environment. Negative people have so much power because they sneak up on us. They start with subtle comments; with secrets, gossip, or complaints about the organization or individuals within it. Many times we don't intend to get caught up in the negativity; we just do. Then, over a short period of time, it becomes infectious and we find ourselves adding to the negativity. Before we know it, we've become a prisoner of negativity—a victim of its subtle powers of captivation. Take new employees, for example. They almost always enter an organization with a positive attitude. The negative person sees them as prey and slowly *helps* them. They inform the "newbie" about the organization's ineffectiveness or the ineffective nature of its management. Soon enough, they capture their victim. It's a tragedy if you think about it, because negative people have the power to destroy dreams and potential. What can you do to avoid the negative individual? Here are a few tips.

- **Understand What Negativity Is.** A negative person isn't someone who comes to you for advice because he or she is struggling with the company or an individual within the company—everyone struggles with company policies or individuals at times. If someone says, "I am really frustrated with this company. I tried to talk to John and he just isn't getting back to me. What do you think I should do?" the person isn't being negative. Rather, he or she is seeking a solution to the problem. In contrast, consider this statement: "I am really frustrated with this company. I talked to John and the guy never gets back to me. He's such an idiot. This entire company is a joke. I'm over this place!" This is clearly a negative statement coming from a negative person. We don't think you should be part of gossip about others or constant complaining about the organization. (For more on how to deal with negative people, see our book *The Canoe Theory*. It's a great resource on the topic of negativity and provides more tips on how to deal with negative people.)

- **Double-Check Yourself.** Think of it this way: if someone was a thief, who would he or she tell? You know the answer; he or she would most likely go to another thief. If someone was looking to share a rude joke or story, who would that person share the joke with? Again, the answer is clear: someone who that person knows will agree with the joke or joke teller. So, you have to ask yourself why negative people come to you. Do they perceive *you* as negative? If they can go to anyone to impart their negativity, why would they choose you? You may want to double-check your own image.

- **Move Away from Negative People.**   This isn't as difficult as you may think. If you don't have much of a relationship with them, you can simply avoid them. Change your patterns: don't eat lunch with them, discontinue your breaks with them, and find reasons why you can't talk or meet. Remember, if you associate with them, silence on negativity is often interpreted as agreement. If negativity is coming from someone you care about, take a different tactic. Ask that person's permission to provide feedback. Then, tell that individual that, in your view, you believe he would be more powerful if negativity were not a part of his behavior.

- **Understand That Negativity Drains Your Power to Excel.**   By focusing on the positive aspects of your organization, you move closer to your own power source. You are guaranteed to improve your sales performance. Negativity, on the other hand, is a major drain. It's a virus that destroys every individual's potential. The time you spend engaged in negative talk about your company is time that you could be spending on building your talent and reputation. In contrast, being positive is a powerful magnet.

- **Realize That All Companies Have Problems.**   Most negative people focus on what's wrong with a company or its management. What you need to realize is that all companies have problems. No organization is perfect, and no company ever will be. We have had the pleasure of working throughout the world with some very high-profile firms. You might imagine they are without issues, but not so. Companies are like relationships: they have good days and not so good days. It's your choice what you focus on. If you focus on the good your organization offers, you will see only the good. If you concentrate on the negative, you sacrifice your own personal power. A negative focus will drain your positive storage tank:

your constructive energy. Give the organization a break (including management!). Realize that if you were in a management position, you too would be a target. You may believe that you would do a better job, but we know that even if you performed well, you would be judged harshly by some. Instead, consider supporting management. If you feel that the company is beyond help, then have the integrity to move on. Find a new organization where you can contribute and be happy, but under no circumstances stay and undermine the integrity of the organization to which you presently belong. It's unfair to your colleagues who are trying to be successful.

- **Understand Why People Are Negative.**   Sometimes people are negative because their own negativity prevents them from excelling. Other times, it's something in their histories, their stories. In most cases, negative people are unable to admit that the *real reason* they don't get ahead is because of their attitudes. The other possibility is they may be getting payoffs for staying negative, such as sympathy for others or proof that they are "right" about their stories.

- **Take a Stand.**   Make a decision to either confront negative people and tell them you can no longer listen when their conversations turn to gossip or negative talk, or move away from them. If you decide to confront them, once again, start by asking for their permission to give feedback. Once you get their permission, tell them that it's not personal, but that you want to move toward the positive. If they get defensive, remember that it's not about you. It's up to them to confront themselves about their own behavior once they calm down. If they judge you harshly (which they may), then you might consider if you want them around you or if you want them as friends. You get to make the decision. You also get to double-check your own attitude and make the decision to gravitate toward people who see the world and its possibilities in a positive light. If the problem of negativity is too complex for you to handle, seek outside advice from someone you trust and who has experience in this area of thinking.

Summary

It's all about your *thoughts* surrounding demand generation. They are what dictate your success. Your beliefs about making net new dials to target prospects or existing clients in new departments are the driving force behind your results. If you have a "story" that you're intruding or being a pest, your attempts fail. Check what beliefs you may have about driving new business.

Key points about mindset:

- Having a proven formula for making net new contacts successfully is critical.
- Salespeople have "stories" (beliefs) that dictate the level of their interest in driving net new business.
- Attaching a meaningful outcome to the work of prospecting creates motivation.
- Finding your "magnet" is the secret to consistency of effort.
- Negative people are dream stealers.
- Your results reveal your story.

CHAPTER

4

PRODUCT KNOWLEDGE

How Much Do You Need to Know Before Dialing?

First, the good news. When a new salesperson begins at an organization, most of the training is devoted to acquiring product knowledge. Rightly so; product knowledge *should* take first priority because it is critically important. Now, the not-so-good news: product knowledge by itself isn't the complete formula for sales success. Much more is involved, including selling mechanics and mindset.

Here's one example of why product knowledge alone isn't sufficient to do the job. When we started in the commercial real estate business, we were sent to San Francisco for one week of training. Although we spent plenty of time in training, because we'd just started, we didn't really know what to concentrate on—it was difficult to determine what information was the most critical since we hadn't been in the field yet. We struggled with connecting the dots. Once we got into the field, we discovered we were unprepared for the challenges presented by commercial real estate. Most of what had been covered in training certainly had value, but it didn't teach us how to survive in the business. Specifically, we weren't taught how to find new business—which in the world of commercial real estate represents almost everything, especially when you are new.

After leaving the industry and forming our own organization, we have now trained thousands of salespeople and, interestingly enough, we find the same situation in most industries. *Salespeople leave corporate training without knowing how to effectively drive net new business.* It's not that the trainers in these companies aren't doing a great job; it's just that some of them have never been in the field of selling, so trainers are often asking a salesperson to do something they haven't done themselves.

We find that the same thing happens at Fortune 500 companies: new salespeople enter the organization and quickly get shipped off to some location for weeks, sometimes even months, for training. What they get is often countless hours of product knowledge instruction with very little focus on driving net new business or how to build their future account base. Again, it frequently has to do with the fact that the instructors may have never carried a sales card.

There's another problem. Despite the fact that organizations spend a great deal of time teaching product knowledge, we are sometimes amazed at the limited product knowledge attendees have. Perhaps it's lack of retention, but we definitely see evidence of product knowledge gaps when we are training SOAR. When it comes to senior attendees in the SOAR program, it's different, because they have figured out what they need to know after years of selling in their industry. As a result, they are often competent at handling objections and selling. The rookies and mid-players are another matter. They consistently get stuck when faced with objections and generally struggle when they have to move the call to the next stage. If questions go much beyond the surface, their incompetency begins to show and, soon enough, the call is lost. Once again, it's not that they didn't get product knowledge when they came to the company, it's just that by the time they get to use it in a selling application, 2 + 2 doesn't always add to 4. (You have to wonder how many opportunities are lost due to poor retention of product knowledge.)

Think about it this way: doctors have to go through years of product knowledge instruction and, once they leave medical school, they must continue spending years in residency, working closely with experienced doctors. Only then will they be considered competent enough to go it alone. Salespeople, on the other hand, complete college, get hired, spend a week or a few months learning about product knowledge, and then are sent to the field to attempt to excel in their sales career. It's really a travesty in the world of selling.

The bottom line is that it's incumbent upon every salesperson to discover the key selling tools needed. There is much more required than what is instructed during initial training. Just as we did in the commercial real estate world, you have to figure it out and determine what you need most and where to get it. You are responsible for adding to your product knowledge bag. If what the company offers isn't enough, seek out someone who is performing well in the organization and have the individual share his or her thoughts about how to succeed in your position.

A Story About the Power of Product Knowledge and High Integrity Selling

We were just building Dialexis and realized we needed a copier that could print professional presentation materials and possibly workbooks. We researched various options and decided to shop at an equipment dealer in our area so we could see multiple manufacturers' product lines. We met with the owner of the dealership and gave him our list of requirements as well as our budget, which was small. He immediately showed us several copiers and said we would be extremely satisfied with any of them. We explained that we wanted reliable performance and that we were occasionally going to use card stock and we didn't want the machine to jam. He then said, "This is the copier for you. In fact, you can take it to your office, use the heavy stock paper, and if you don't like it, you can bring it back." So we wrote him a check and headed back to the office, looking forward to using the new machine.

Well, within days we were frustrated and upset. The copier jammed constantly when we used the heavy stock. We called the salesperson we purchased it from and he said, "It may do that at times, but it's a good copier." After a few more days of disappointment, we decided to return the machine. Now we needed to find another dealer. We looked through more local dealers before realizing that we hadn't considered Xerox. So we gave them a call and asked to see a salesperson as soon as possible. We were immediately contacted and subsequently scheduled an appointment. Before the Xerox salesperson arrived, we agreed that we would not spend over $3,000. When we met the salesperson, we stated our expectations and expressed our frustrations with the equipment we had purchased from the previous dealer. We asked the salesperson if Xerox had anything that would work within our price range.

Now, this is where product knowledge and selling integrity really made an impact on us (and our buying decision)—so much so that we still remember this experience 20 years later. The Xerox salesperson explained that, in order to print the heavier stock that we wanted to use, we would have to purchase a copier that was significantly more expensive. He said to do what we wanted to do would require a purchase in the price range of $75,000! He went on to explain that he began his career as a technician and had repaired and seen more copiers than most, and he knew for a fact that the type of paper we wanted to use required a sophisticated printer. Because of his extensive product knowledge—specifically, his know-how and experience with a wide array of copiers—he was able to show us options within our price range and give us honest assessments of their features. We decided to purchase a Xerox copier that was well over our budget, but that would perform reliably and meet our needs. That afternoon we wrote a check for $6,500—and we did it with pleasure!

That Xerox purchase was one of the best investments of our early business career. In fact, after using it for five years, we sold it to an attorney for $3,000! We still talk about what a great salesperson we had. He wasn't a slick fast talker. Instead, he was someone who simply knew his product. He didn't *sell* us, he *educated* us and, without pressure, he demonstrated amazing product knowledge. It was truly a pleasure to buy from a Xerox professional.

Your Responsibility As a Sales Professional

You wouldn't want a doctor to suggest you take medication or have an operation if you thought the doctor had limited product knowledge, would you? It's no different for a salesperson. You give advice, recommend solutions, and represent yourself as a competent professional. It's a grave responsibility, because your recommendations often carry significant downside for a client if you give the wrong advice.

Unfortunately, salespeople are often allowed to represent a company before they are truly ready. There are too many salespeople who are simply after the commission, and despite the fact they are not qualified to diagnose or recommend a responsible solution, they do. *Don't let that be you.* If you learn beyond what your company has provided, you will help yourself and your clients immensely. Also keep in mind that, when something is beyond your capabilities, you can bring in other resources that may be available to you, such as an engineer, your sales manager, your marketing expert, or a senior salesperson. The bottom line is, product knowledge matters, and you need to do everything you can to get it. Get competent or bring a competent partner or colleague on calls that require deeper product knowledge until you can answer all the questions—it will pay off in loyalty from your clients in the future. You will also be able to sleep better at night. You will represent what we so admire: *a true professional* in the world of sales. Our view is that salespeople are responsible for leaving every call better than they found it. That means be honest, know your business, and always do what is best for your prospect. Operating from this foundation will mean you will have a long and rewarding career in sales.

Here is another perspective on product knowledge. Let's say that the best product knowledge rating is a 10 and the worst is a 1. Now, if you are calling on a prospect that has a product knowledge rating of 5 in your field, what do you think your product knowledge rating would have to be that is acceptable to that prospect? The answer is 5! Surprised? Think of it this way: if you are calling on a person who has a product knowledge rating of 10, what do you think that person would want? If you said a 10, we're going to suggest you think again. In our view, a 5 will accept a 5, but a person who is a 10 wants *above* a 10. People who have exceptional product knowledge don't want to learn what they already know; they want to learn something new. A 5 will be satisfied with another 5, but the 10 wants it all. The moral of the story is, when you are calling on someone that you think knows his or her stuff, you'd better be prepared by having a pro with you—that is, until you become the expert!

Who Is Responsible for Providing Product Knowledge?

Your company, of course, is responsible for providing product knowledge, but as we have said, that doesn't preclude you from completing the task. We once met someone at an event who was in sales for a company that he had been with for about one year. We asked him how he liked working for the company, and he replied, "it's OK." When we asked why he said it was just "OK," he said, "they don't train us." We asked what training he had been given, and he said he was sent to three weeks of training, but that he didn't think it was very good. We asked what he expected and what he thought the solution was, and he said *he really didn't know.* We hear this frequently, so we were not surprised at his response. What left us dumbfounded was that the thought of seeking out training, no matter what type, hadn't even occurred to him. It's the company's responsibility to provide basic training, but they may not provide *all* the training you may need. Training departments in most companies do a great job, however, once the company provides the initial training for any new salesperson, even a senior salesperson, it's every salesperson's responsibility to get what else may be needed to be successful and stay on top.

How to Speed Up Your Product Knowledge Learning

Again, the bottom line is that you have the opportunity and you are responsible for seeking out training beyond what the company provides. It's incumbent upon you to dig into the organization, ask senior salespeople what they feel is important, ask your sales manager how you can find more information, or reach out to other departments. Talk to the senior salespeople. In fact, ask them as many questions as you can. They usually love to give advice, so take advantage of their experience. You can't stop learning product knowledge, ever! You need to accelerate your learning; becoming competent doesn't have to take years. You can speed up the process as fast as you want—and you should. Seek as much product knowledge as possible in the shortest amount of time. Remember, the more competent you become, the more successful you will be. Plus, it's an amazing feeling to know that you can serve the client's best interests when the opportunity is at your doorstep.

Summary

Key points about product knowledge:

- Product knowledge matters if you expect to be considered a trusted advisor.
- Personality or jokes won't make up for poor product knowledge; organizations want sales experts.
- Your organization will provide basic product knowledge, but getting to the deeper stuff is up to you.
- Speed up your product knowledge by seeking assistance from your organization's best salespeople or sales leaders.
- Rookies don't have to know everything, but they have to connect with someone who does when necessary.

CHAPTER

5

UNDERSTANDING THE RECEPTIONIST: THE NIZ ZONE

Receptionists Aren't the Enemy

It's interesting to hear what salespeople think of receptionists during SOAR instruction. Most of the time we hear the same thing: "they're trying to shut you down" or "they're trying to block you" or even,"they're lying." The list goes on. We often find the same statements coming from sales managers

Here is what we found to be true: when salespeople believe that the receptionist is out to block them, *they end up creating that result.* As discussed in Chapter 3, it is our experience that what a salesperson believes is ultimately what he or she creates. Rather than see the receptionist as the enemy, salespeople now have the opportunity to understand that they have the full power to professionally breeze past the receptionist. The path is to simply follow SOAR principles and strategies.

Creating Your Results

I (Dave) hold the belief that I can find a parking place anywhere anytime. What's interesting about this is, it doesn't matter to me if it's Game 6 of the World Series and the sign outside the parking lot says "Lot Full." I just don't accept "lot full" as my reality. My reality is, "there is always an open spot!" And guess where that open spot is in my reality? Usually, front row right near the entry! That's simply where I believe the open spot is . . . and that's usually the spot that I find. This is true where we live, in Laguna Beach, California, a tourist haven. When my wife and I decide to go to one of our favorite restaurants in Laguna, we generally head into the maze of cars and I ask her where she wants to park. Knowing what I believe, she usually suggests right in front of the restaurant. So, I get my mindset ready. I start thinking the *universe* will deliver my parking space and visualize that a spot will appear right in front of the restaurant. Even if the traffic is terrible and 80 percent of the drivers are seeking a parking place, it doesn't faze me. I know I will create a spot in front of the restaurant. Guess what? I get it. Even if a car pulls in front of me at the last minute, I know it was simply so my spot shows up at the right time. I know I can get a parking place, and it's my mindset, my way of thinking, that supports me in making it happen.

The Receptionist Is a Challenge, Not a Block

So what does this have to do with getting past the receptionist? It's very simple: believing you will be blocked by the receptionist *creates* being blocked by the receptionist. Receptionists are *not* there to block you—rather, *you* block you.

As we said, whenever we train salespeople, we often ask what they think the receptionist's job is. The familiar reply is, "they are there to block you." As we mentioned, from our perspective, it's not that way at all. As a matter of fact we see it as a *neutral event*. Our thought is, the receptionist is simply doing a job by answering the telephone! No more, no less. When calling a company, salespeople first encounter the receptionist, and because they don't handle the contact with the receptionist well or the questions the receptionist asks effectively, they often fail to reach the decision maker they want to reach. They interpret the situation as being blocked when, in fact, it's not the receptionist who blocked the salesperson, it's the lack of technique that's the culprit.

As we said, the receptionist is just doing a job, and if you work with the receptionist and follow exactly the information SOAR teaches (more on this shortly), blocking becomes a nonissue and your call will go through. To us the receptionist is not the enemy. Instead, the receptionist is simply a professional sales call challenge.

We are certainly aware that some receptionists screen and some don't. Those that screen calls and ask the tough questions are the ones that you need smart SOAR answers for! Unfortunately, most salespeople don't have the right answers; as a result they get frustrated because they don't know how to get past the difficult questions many receptionists ask. Sometimes salespeople even stretch the truth or become rude because they just don't know what to do when they get challenged at the entry level of a corporation. Often when they get stuck they just hang up!

We mentioned that beginning your calls with a belief that the receptionist is out to block you only brings blocking. Why not shift your thinking from the mindset of, "I am being blocked," to "The receptionist is just doing a job—I will get through!"

The NIZ Zone

Some of the articles we've read about gatekeepers recommend that you always be polite to the receptionist and tell her why you are calling. We agree, you should always be polite. *But you have to use extreme caution when you are asked why you are calling.* That doesn't mean lie. It means use SOAR.

When you're talking to a receptionist you are in what we refer to as the "NIZ: No Information Zone." Not that you can't get information or that the receptionist doesn't have information; the NIZ zone means you are in a place where you shouldn't give any more information than you are asked! Essentially, the more you talk the more you *are in jeopardy* in the NIZ zone. Less is more. For example, you know that when a person is deposed by an attorney he is being coached by his attorney to say as little as possible when he is questioned. For example, if the opposing attorney asks, "Where were you Friday night at 8 p.m.?" you aren't supposed to say, "I was at home, but I stopped by the gun store on my way there." That's a crazy example, but you get the point. You only answer what you are asked, using as few words as possible: "I was at home."

Let's compare the deposition situation to the NIZ zone of a corporation. You phone a company on a prospecting call and the receptionist answers, "American Products." You respond by saying, "Bill Smith, please." The receptionist replies by asking, "Who's calling?"

You respond with, "Sandra Olson of ABC company." Now let's pause a moment. Notice that the receptionist *didn't* say, "Who's calling *and* what company are you with?" That is what you *thought* the receptionist asked. In fact, the receptionist just asked for your name by asking, "Who is calling?" It wasn't necessary for you to provide the name of your firm. All you needed to do was answer the question "Who's calling?" by replying with your name.

Why is this so important? Because when you say more than you need to you put yourself at risk of getting disconnected. When you provide your company name when it wasn't necessary, a receptionist may know of your product and then say, "No, thank you, we're not interested." In many smaller companies, the receptionist may be the brother, sister, mother, daughter, wife, and so forth of the boss, and any one of these people may feel at liberty to shut you out quickly without further questions. All it takes is you stating the name of your company, and he or she may make a decision that you are selling something. If your company's name doesn't reveal the nature of your product, you are still in danger because the receptionist may ask, "What does your company do?"

We understand there can be mitigating factors, but why take the risk of providing your company without being asked? You are in the NIZ zone: the more you give the less you get. (Don't confuse the receptionist zone with a call to the president's executive assistant; when you are in the NIZ zone, be cautious.)

"Chip Talk:" The Preprogrammed Mind of the Receptionist

When employees are hired who are expected to interface with customers, they are taught how to *engage* with those customers. For example, when you order coffee at Starbucks the person helping you will always ask, "room for cream?" Or, if you are at a McDonald's, they ask, "would you like fries with that?" The same thing happens when you call a company. The receptionist asks the typical question, "what is this regarding?" "is he/she expecting your call?" or "what company are you calling from?" We think of these questions as "chip talk." In other words, it's as if a chip with preprogrammed questions and responses has been installed in the mind of the receptionist when he or she is hired.

After a while on the job, the questions the receptionist is trained to ask no longer carry the same importance. Those preprogrammed questions have been asked so many times that the receptionist asking those questions may not even aware he or she is asking them!

Chip Story

We were waiting in line at Starbucks coffee with two people ahead of us. The first guy ordered a regular large coffee and the server said "room for cream?" The guy said no. The next guy in front of us said he wanted a decaf coffee and the server said, "room for cream?" He replied, no. When we stepped up to place our order, we said, "We would like two Grande coffees *with room for cream please.*" The server handed us our coffee, we took it over to the cream area, opened the top and—you guessed it—no room for cream! We laughed and remarked to one another that if we were to go back to the server and ask what had happened, the server would simply say "I'm sorry, I guess I didn't hear you ask for cream." The question, "room for cream?" is so unconscious and programmed that this server has no idea any longer that she/he is even asking the question! People ask these questions because they were told to do so when they were first hired, but after a while the questions no longer have meaning. As a matter of fact, we know that they don't even realize they are asking the question.

Over thousands of live calls made by corporate salespeople, we have clear evidence that receptionists really don't really want the answers to many of the questions they ask. Most of the questions asked by receptionists are "coming from the chip." Now, this isn't to say that receptionists aren't smart or they aren't good at what they do, this is simply an observation. What you need to know as a salesperson is that the majority of receptionists ask questions "from their chip," and if you don't "trigger" the chip in the wrong way, you will get through. In the end, it's like a game. The receptionist moves left; you move right. You answer the receptionist's questions in a strategic way so that you can get through to the person you want to talk to.

Death Questions: How You Get Blocked

When researching why salespeople struggle so hard at reaching decision makers on the telephone, we found most get stuck when interacting with the receptionist. The fundamental problem is due to answering the receptionist's "chip" questions incorrectly (we call them *death questions* because when the receptionist's questions are answered incorrectly by the salesperson the call is terminated; it dies.) What do you think the four most common questions are that cause a salesperson to get stuck on the way to the decision maker? Here is a list of the questions we have found to be the most common:

1. "What is this regarding?"

2. "Is he/she expecting your call?"

3. "What is the name of your company?"

4. "Is this a sales call?"

("Do you have an appointment?" is asked when making *live* street calls, but not so much on the telephone.)

We call these questions death questions because if a salesperson answers them wrong in the receptionist NIZ zone, the call dies and the salesperson loses a potential opportunity! (Remember, NIZ stands for No Information Zone. That means don't give information you don't have to give; as we said, the more you give the less you usually get.) Now you get to answer another question: what information do you think is on the receptionist's chip? If you said the questions above, you are right! Look at the following call example to understand how a net new prospecting call typically happens.

Call Example

Receptionist: American Products Company.

Salesperson: Bill Smith, please.

Receptionist: Who is calling? (*not a death question*)

Salesperson: Mary Johnson.

Receptionist: May I ask what this is regarding? (*death question!*)

Salesperson: I am with ABC Company and I wanted to speak to Bill about the company's marketing platform. (*big mistake . . . caught by the death question!*)

When the receptionist asked the death question, the salesperson gave the receptionist more details than he needed to. The receptionist asked the death question, "What is this regarding?" because it was on the chip, and the salesperson answered it innocently enough, but incorrectly! The salesperson told the truth, which salespeople should, but he doesn't have to answer the question the way he did. The mistake was made by the salesperson despite the fact that he answered the question the only way he knew how. There is a better answer that doesn't set off the chip! Using the SOAR formula, the salesperson can say, "Just let [the executive you are calling] know it's regarding [insert your full name]."

Answers to Death Questions

This response might surprise you. (This is one place where you can benefit from getting off your *dot*.) As we mentioned earlier, we have seen thousands of live dials made to every conceivable industry, title, and position in over a dozen cultures and our advice about how to answer "death questions" really works. It works so well that, when the first dialer makes a call in the course of a live SOAR program and uses the exact responses we provide, people in the class have to contain themselves from gasping out loud! (Remember, we are talking about the receptionist, not the executive assistant to the president. Responding to death questions with the EAP is not a problem; you simply tell the assistant why you are calling because you are speaking to a strong high influencer. (You will read more about how to respond to the executive assistant later in the book.)

Call Example

Receptionist: American Products Company.

Salesperson: Bill Smith, please

Receptionist: Who's calling? (*not a death question*)

Salesperson: Mary Johnson.

Receptionist: May I ask what this is regarding? (*death question!*)

Salesperson: Just let him know it's regarding Mary Johnson.

Possible Receptionist Response #1: Just a moment (*puts you through*)

OR (Here is another response to a further death question)

Possible Receptionist Response #2: And he'll know who Mary Johnson is?

Salesperson: I'm sure if you mention Mary Johnson, it'll be fine.

OK, now let's examine what we have just told you, because we are sure you are confused or may disagree. Although it seems odd to say, "just let [him/her] know it's regarding Mary Johnson (your name), it works! The receptionist has asked, "what is this *regarding*?" and your answer works because you are *repeating the word that is most important to the receptionist* (which is, "regarding") so when you say, "just let [him/her] know it's *regarding* Mary Johnson," it just works! The receptionist ends up putting you through. Oddly enough, the receptionist doesn't think it's strange that you answered, "Just let [him/her] know" it's "regarding" *you (your name)*.

We know the reason receptionists put you through despite the fact it seems illogical is that the question, "what is this regarding?" is really just a chip question *and it has been answered*. In most cases, receptionists really *don't want to know* or *don't care what it's regarding* as long as they have an answer and it doesn't "hit the chip" wrong.

In live classes, most of the participants aren't sure it will work, but every time the first "live dialer" uses this technique and ultimately flies past the receptionist and gets through to a decision maker or someone of high influence, there are high-fives around the room and we hear statements like, "OMG, it worked, I can't believe it!"

As we mentioned earlier, in small companies the receptionist may often be a family member and that person may have more of a sense of authority to challenge you. In larger organizations it's much easier to pass by the receptionist if you follow these suggestions. It's important to follow these instructions exactly as they are stated so you don't crash and burn before you even get a shot at the CEO!

With regards to the second receptionist challenge, ... "and he'll know who Mary Johnson is?" and your response, *"I'm sure if you mention Mary Johnson it'll be fine,"* this works as well. Receptionists almost always put you through because, once again, it's a chip question and you have answered it. Note: another reason we know it will always be fine is because after making thousands of live calls, our research shows it is always fine!

Example of Death Questions That Require the Same Response

Receptionist: What is this regarding?

Salesperson: Just let [him/her] know it's regarding [your name].

Receptionist: Is she expecting your call?

Salesperson: Just let her know it's regarding [your name].

Receptionist: Is this a sales call?

Salesperson: Just let [him/her] know it's regarding [your name].

Receptionist: What company are you with?

Salesperson: Just let [him/her] know it's regarding [your name].

Receptionist: Tell me more.

Salesperson: Just let [him/her] know it's regarding [your name].

In summary, any of the death questions will be easily handled by those two responses, and, as a matter of fact, no matter what the question is, you can use the responses we have suggested and you will find yourself getting past the receptionist with ease. Only upon rare exception are you likely to be blocked. If you follow the script *exactly* and have the right mindset in place, you are more than likely going to succeed in making contact!

The key is to stay on the call until you make contact. It requires strong intention; we call it "Riding the Bull." That means attempting to reach at least four contacts before you hang up. A bull rider stays on the bull for eight seconds at the rodeo. We want salespeople to be as determined as if they were riding a bull on every net new call; that is, to stay on the call until they have made four attempts. Attempt one is connecting to the president; attempt two is connecting to the EAP; and attempts three and four are contacting two other high influencers who can assist you with information that supports reaching the decision maker. That's called riding the bull.

In smaller companies, you may only be able to ride the bull one or two deep because they don't have that many employees. In the end, it is really your determination to make contact that matters.

There is another strategy for answering difficult questions. It's called "bridge and shift." Have you ever noticed that when politicians or public figures are asked a question, they don't always answer the exact question that was asked? They don't lie; they just answer the question *the way they want to answer it*. Essentially, what they do is "bridge and shift."

Let's say that, during a press session at the White House, a reporter asks, "Mr. President, is it true that you gave your daughter a high-paying job at the White House?" The president replies to the reporter, "Let me say this: I believe we are fair with all our hiring policies, just as I know we are being fair in Afghanistan. Next question." The reporter sits down and says to another reporter, "How did we get into Afghanistan? What happed to my question about his daughter getting a high-paying job?"

This is not to say the president lied; he didn't. He just *bridged and shifted*. So, what you need to understand as a salesperson is that you don't always have to answer the question being asked by the receptionist. Now, if you are asked the same question three times, then you have no other option but to answer the exact question being asked. However, most salespeople give the information immediately and sometimes without the question being asked or thinking how they can "bridge and shift," and as a result, the receptionist blocks the salesperson.

Receptionist Answers That Mislead You: Keyword Listening

Listening and making contact with a decision maker go hand-in-hand. At least half of the reasons salespeople do not make contact or get more appointments has to do with inadequate listening skills. Let's take a look at a few examples in Figure 5-1 of how keyword listening changes the game when you are involved with demand generation. We know that if you want to make contact, small listening details matter.

When you look at the keywords shown in bold under "Statement," you can see the potential for lost opportunity due to not picking up on

Statement:	Incorrect Assumption:	Salesperson Action:
"I don't **believe** he is in"	He is not in	Hang up and call back
"He isn't **available**"	He can't talk now	Hang up and call back
"The **timing** isn't right"	It's a bad time	Call back in the future
"**Right now** isn't a good time"	They aren't willing to listen	Don't push—call back
"Not interested **at the moment**"	They aren't interested	Sell, sell, sell
"Perhaps sometime in the **future**"	Sounds like a lead	Hang up—call in 6 months
"We're **pretty happy** with . . ."	They are happy	Sell, sell, sell
"We're **working with** . . .	We are better	Sell, sell, sell
"Call us **next quarter**"	Prospect!	Call next quarter
"We looked at your proposal and **most** thought it was good"	It's a deal, or very close	Put in the pipeline

Figure 5-1 *Keyword Listening Chart: The WRONG Way to Keyword Listen*

Statement:	Better Assumption:	Salesperson Action:
"I don't **believe** he is in"	He **may** be in	Page or clarify "**believe**"
"He isn't **available**"	He **may** be available	Page or clarify "**available**"
"The **timing** isn't right"	The timing **may** be right	Clarify "**timing**"
"**Right now** isn't a good time"	It may actually be a good time	Question "**right now**"
"Not interested **at the moment**"	This could be a lead	Clarify "**at the moment**"
"Perhaps sometime in the **future**"	This could be a lead	Clarify "**future**"
"We're **pretty happy** with . . ."	Not completely happy	Clarify "**pretty**"
"We're **working with** . . ."	We are better	Clarify "**working with**"
"Call us **next quarter**"	This could be a lead	Clarify why "**next quarter**"
"We looked at your proposal and **most** thought it was good"	Someone didn't like it	Clarify "**most**"

Figure 5-2 *Keyword Listening Chart: The RIGHT Way to Keyword Listen*

the keywords in the response. Let's look at the examples in Figure 5-2 and how the call could have been handled differently.

You can see the difference when you catch the keywords in any statement, particularly on a prospecting call. But this is also true for any call, including a call where you have a relationship with the client. It's amazing to watch salespeople hang up or make an assumption when they are working so hard to (a) reach someone or (b) gain an understanding of a conversation, or simply because they didn't clarify a keyword that was said. Questioning a keyword can change the results dramatically on any call. The same thing applies when you reach your target contact or even during a face-to-face appointment. Keywords are presented all the time on calls, and many of them slip right by the salesperson! Over and over again, salespeople leave a meeting or hang up from a call believing there is no interest because they missed the keywords placed right in front of them. Hearing the keyword could have opened up the opportunity!

We were delivering the SOAR formula to a group of very senior salespeople, and when we were explaining "keyword listening," one of the executives in the back of the room said, "Wow, I can use this anywhere!" He explained, "I have been missing this guy I'm trying to contact. Now I have a better chance of connecting. I'm sure I haven't been hearing the keywords!"

Oddly enough, keywords are rarely missed in our personal lives, it's just in the business sector where we fail to pick up on them. If you begin to listen differently, you will start to hear keywords and you will begin to serve your client, your company, and your own results noticeably. Try doing it today; really pay attention to the keywords that are being said to you in nearly every conversation you have. In Chapter 9, you will find the best way to clarify keywords and objections since they are often bundled together.

Remember your *story*; is it possible you don't keyword listen in business because you think you don't want to know the answer? Are you assuming that the information you will hear isn't what you want to hear? Before all calls, ground yourself so you know *why* you are making the call and what results you are committed to achieve.

When you are driving net new business, you may not always get a death question from the receptionist when you ask for the target contact, but you will get other questions and, if you are not paying attention to your response, you may get disconnected or put through to voice mail when you didn't need to. Here are a few examples of the answers receptionists give and suggestions for responding while keyword listening.

Call Example

Receptionist: ABC Company.

Salesperson: Mary Smith, please.

Receptionist: Who is calling?

Salesperson: John Stevens.

Receptionist: I don't believe she is in. (*The keyword is believe, so you would ask to page.*)

or

Receptionist: She isn't available. (*The keyword is available.*)

When the receptionist says, "she isn't available," you need to clarify the meaning of "available." You would say something like, "when you say she is not *available*, do you mean she is out of the office?" "in a meeting?" "traveling?" "away from her desk?" and so on. You may be surprised by the response from the receptionist when you clarify what the keyword "available" means. The receptionist frequently says something like, "well, I haven't seen her today." That doesn't mean she isn't in! It's a *lazy* response, but not because the receptionist is lazy. Receptionists are often really busy—people checking in for meetings, five lines ringing, three callers asking questions, and that's all happening at the same time. So, when we say lazy, it's more that it's an easy response.

Most receptionists want to connect you, and unfortunately it's usually to voice mail. When you are speaking to the receptionist, it's like the game called "hot potato." Receptionists often just want to get rid of the potato, but in this case it's you, the caller. A receptionist wants to move you through the call and to whoever you're calling as soon as possible, so when you are trying to make contact and the receptionist responds by saying, "Mary isn't available," that doesn't mean she isn't in the office! It also doesn't mean that the receptionist is lying, it may just be an assumptive statement by the receptionist that may not be *fact*. The only way you will know is by qualifying that statement.

Call Example

Receptionist: I haven't seen her today.

Again, the statement doesn't mean she isn't in; it simply means the receptionist hasn't seen her today. You need to hear the *keyword* or *phrase* and clarify its meaning before you hang up or get put through to voice mail.

Receptionist: She is not in her office.

Again, this doesn't mean she isn't available; maybe she is getting coffee!

Receptionist: Would you like her voice mail?

This is an interesting reply from receptionists, because it is that "bridge and shift" response we mentioned earlier. Think about it: you asked for Mary and the receptionist jumped to a nonanswer reply. Imagine if you asked me for a pencil and I replied, "would you like a cup of coffee?" Wouldn't you find that odd! So why do you accept this kind of reply from a receptionist and hang up or leave a voice mail? *Don't.* You never received an answer to the question you asked that made sense, so respond accordingly.

Summary

Understanding how a receptionist is wired matters. Receptionists are not lying in wait to block salespeople. They are simply doing their job by asking appropriate questions of the caller. Making up a story that all receptionists are the enemy won't serve a salesperson.

Key points about understanding the receptionist and the NIZ zone:

- Receptionists don't block salespeople. Salespeople block themselves.
- Don't give more information then you are asked when you're in the NIZ zone.
- Keyword listening is critical.
- Receptionists are "chipped"; that is, they always ask the questions that they were originally told to ask when they were hired. The fact is, they may not even care what your answer is as long as it doesn't hit the chip wrong.
- Ride the Bull until you have executed the SOAR process. That means, attempt to reach four key people before disconnecting if possible if the CEO is not available.
- Receptionists often respond to your question with words or statements that require qualifying, such as, "Bill isn't 'available.'" The receptionist's response that Bill isn't available doesn't mean Bill isn't available.

CHAPTER

6

RIDE THE BULL: GET TO THE POWER ZONE!

The Power Zone: PZ

The SOAR formula requires salespeople to begin their contact process by reaching what SOAR calls the *Power Zone (PZ)*. That often takes *Riding the Bull* in order to get past the receptionist (who dwells in the *NIZ: no information zone*). The power zone is where the president *and* the executive assistant to the president (EAP) reside. We refer to it as "the power zone" because, essentially, it's where salespeople get power!

As we covered in Chapter 5, riding the bull simply means staying on the call for four attempts at reaching a decision maker or high influencer (just as a bull rider stays on the bull for eight seconds.) The live call portion of SOAR when participants "ride the bull" usually causes a great deal of tension. It takes courage to step up to the dialing desk; the calls are on speakerphone and everyone in the program can hear. Admiration for those that are first to dial brings forth a resounding applause. Remember, this has been a concept in the class until the proof of concept moment, but now salespeople are proving the concept by actually using the material and dialing live. Attendees come to the dialing chair tentative and often scared out of their minds (yes, even the big senior gorillas are tense), but somehow they find the courage to take the risk. It's a bit like a bungee jump. The moment you step on the diving platform, you ask yourself, "what was I thinking?" But before you can think any further, you jump and your life flashes before your eyes! For many, that is what it's like to dial live in front of other salespeople using the SOAR process.

The EAP

Despite the fact that most salespeople usually contact someone other than the company president, we know it's the president *and* the EAP who have power. Even if the president isn't the one handling the decision related to a salesperson's call, the president obviously has exceptional referral power. If a salesperson connects with the president and the president says, "I don't handle that, you need to speak to

John Smith," (because John Smith has P&L responsibility), you have just received a strong referral. When you reach John Smith's office and the assistant says, "what is this regarding?" you can say, "Just let him know that [the president] recommended I speak to him." That's a strong endorsement to an assistant or even John Smith himself! As a result, you'll usually get through.

In most cases, there is a strong possibility of reaching the president. This is especially true of the smaller accounts, where you have a shot at reaching the president or owner of the firm quite frequently. The only area this isn't true is with the Fortune 500 firms; there, you generally have a minimal chance of reaching the actual CEO— but you do have an excellent chance of reaching the EAP. Many salespeople believe EAPs aren't worth contacting because they don't make the decisions, However, EAPs do have very compelling referral power. When you think about it, the EAP sits next to the president in the Power Zone and generally has the attention of the president. If an EAP suggests to the president that she should see you, the president may take the recommendation because she respects her EAP. Even if the president won't see you or the EAP tells you that the president doesn't handle what you are calling about, the EAP will refer you to the decision maker you should be speaking to. Once again, the EAP's referral is significant. The odds of you making contact are greatly improved by going to the PZ rather than asking the receptionist to directly transfer you to the person you think you want.

In our experience, executive assistants are among the best when it comes to professionally representing the president's office. We have consistently found them to be excellent listeners while possessing professional attitudes. Most important, they have the power to direct, and that referral gets results.

A True Story About Using SOAR on a EAP

Several years ago, a friend of ours purchased six patio chairs for his home deck from a well-known retailer with locations throughout Southern California. He wanted all six chairs in black, but the retail outlets of this popular chain didn't have six black chairs at one single location. As a result, he had to drive to four separate locations over several miles to pick up the chairs until he had collected all six. Once he got home, he was dismayed to discover that the chairs required more assembly than he had expected. After working through the night, he finally assembled all six chairs. Proudly, he placed them on his patio and invited his wife out to show her how great they looked.

After two days of using the chairs, he noticed that the wood began to split; not just on one chair, but several. Frustrated, he decided to return the chairs. He called the retailer and explained what had happened. The manager at the store said they would accept the chairs back; all he had to do was bring them to the store. He explained that the chairs were now assembled and he couldn't bring them back in his car since not even a single chair would fit. He asked the manager if they would pick them up. The store manager said it was not their policy to pick the product up, but again stated they would take the chairs back as long as he brought them into the store. He suggested that he could rent a truck from a rental company and bring the chairs back if the store would simply pay for the truck ($100). The manager refused. Our friend then contacted the regional manager and explained his circumstances. He got the same answer. When we heard the story, we suggested he use SOAR. He called back and, with the cooperation of the executive assistant, reached the CEO. The CEO was appalled and immediately agreed to have the chairs picked up and a refund granted. Another example of EAP power and professionalism!

A Note on Death
Questions in the Power Zone

When you are speaking with the receptionist in the no information zone (NIZ), you don't have the referral power from the power zone so you are left dealing with the death questions using the responses suggested in Chapter 5. It's important you know that the only time you need to use those death question responses is when you are in the NIZ, speaking with the receptionist. *We do not recommend those answers to the death questions when you are in the power zone.* The EAP will ask similar questions to the receptionist's, such as, "what is this regarding?" or "is he/she expecting your call?" or "what company are you with?" *but you should use specific responses for the EAP in the power zone* as provided in the example below. (We think of the "hunt trac" as the process of "hunting" for the target you are calling.)

Hunt Trac Call Example

EAP: Bill Smith's office, this is JJ

Salesperson: Is Bill in?

(Use the name as it is given: if the EAP answers, "Bill Smith's office," then say, "is Bill in?" rather than referring to the president as "Mr. Smith.")

EAP: He's on a lengthy conference call, was he expecting your call?

Salesperson: Are you Bill's executive assistant?

EAP: Yes, I am.

Salesperson: Great! Maybe you can help me. My name is [your name] and I am with [your company's name], and the reason I was calling Bill was [state your value statement].

EAP: Let me stop you there. Bill doesn't handle that; you would need to speak to [name of contact]. Let me connect you.

Once you are connected, you can let the person know that you were speaking to JJ in Bill Smith's office and he/she recommended that the two of you speak. Not many people are going to turn you down when you are referred by the president's EAP.

If the president or the EAP is not available, you need to ride the bull and attempt to reach one or two more high influencers if the company is large enough.

Let's get back to riding the bull and the process of attempting to reach Bill or Bill's EAP when you are starting out in the power zone (PZ). This is how the conversation *could go* if you are riding the bull with the receptionist and using the SOAR Hunt Trac.

Receptionist: American Products.

Salesperson: Bill Smith, please

Receptionist: I don't believe he is in. (*the keyword is believe*)

Salesperson: Can you page him please? (*good job hearing the keyword!*)

Receptionist: I haven't seen him today. (*doesn't mean he isn't in*)

Salesperson: Why don't we try paging anyway just to check?

Receptionist: I'm sorry, he didn't answer.

Salesperson: Who *sits near* Bill who might be able to see if he is in the area? (*ride the bull!*)

Receptionist: I don't know, sir, he is in another building.

Salesperson: In the event he is out, what is his business cell number? Perhaps I can reach him there.

Receptionist: I wouldn't have that number.

Salesperson: Who would? (*great keyword listening!*)

Here's another way the conversation could go when it comes to requesting a cell number:

Receptionist: We don't give cell numbers out.

Salesperson: I understand. Why don't I hold while you connect me (*still on the bull!*)

Receptionist: I'm sorry, but I can't do that.

Salesperson: I understand. Why don't we try Bill's executive assistant?

Receptionist: Just a moment.

Receptionist: I'm sorry, Bill's assistant didn't answer.

Salesperson: Let's try paging? (*still on the bull!*)

If this process doesn't lead you to Bill or Bill's EAP, then you still ride the bull and attempt to reach a high influencer. The length of a bull ride will be determined by your call style, your intention, and the patience of the receptionist (it will also depend on the personality of the receptionist, something at which we will look closely in Chapter 7).

Summary

Key points about riding the bull and getting into the power zone:

- Before the call, be intent on "getting in," "making contact."
- Get intentional about achieving an appointment *before* you actually dial.
- Keyword listen, which will help you make contact.
- Get to the Power Zone (the president's office).
- Realize that the EAP (executive assistant to the president) has power to influence.
- You don't have to *reach* a decision maker to ultimately *get to* a decision maker: it's critical to reach a high influencer if your decision maker is 100 percent unavailable.
- Hanging up once you are put through to voice mail, or hanging up because a receptionist made statements you interpret to be fatal to your call, is a huge mistake—riding the bull means using the SOAR formula to make contact.

THE CRITICAL VALUE
STATEMENT

Value Statement vs. Value Proposition

SOAR was created so that salespeople could make contact with decision makers and high influencers. As we began to teach SOAR, we discovered something startling: once salespeople made contact during the live dialing segment of SOAR, *they didn't always know what to say.* That really shocked us. Of course, the salespeople said *something,* but what they said was usually not very compelling. (Part of the problem may have been that they were so surprised that they were able to reach who they wanted to speak to that it was a bit of a jolt when the person actually answered.) After the call, when the instructor would ask what happened and why the salesperson gave such a weak response, the salesperson would simply reply, "I don't know, I just got stuck!"

After we witnessed salesperson after salesperson get stuck on the initial call, we woke up to the fact that salespeople were also in need of value statement support. We found value *propositions* were discussed in corporate trainings, but *value propositions* and *value statements* are not the same thing. The distinction is this: the value statement is a 15- to 30-second introduction, or "elevator pitch," during a telephone call when a salesperson attempts to create instant interest. Value statements may also be referred to as a creative statement, hook statement, opening statement, or elevator statement. In our view, a value *proposition* consists of what a salesperson presents during the subsequent call or face-to-face meeting.

We discovered two key reasons why the brief value statements weren't being developed within the organization. Here are our two big discoveries:

1. In our view, most organizations are not focused on the front end of the prospecting cycle, instead they think from a "once in" perspective. As a result, they tend to teach value proposition training, but not value statement training. As we said, the

value proposition is much more in-depth than a value statement. When salespeople are making initial contact on the telephone; they ordinarily have a very limited opportunity to say something. They don't have time to have the extensive conversation a value proposition entails.

2. There seems to be an assumption that, because salespeople were experienced when they joined the company, they would know what to say once they made contact on an initial call. (The label "experienced" didn't have a period of time associated with it; "experienced" could mean 20 years or 2 years of previous selling history.) Salespeople were given product knowledge during training, and oftentimes it seems companies believe that is sufficient. Certainly, organizations provide more than just product knowledge, but that is generally the primary focus. Not only have we discovered that the opposite is true—that someone with 5 years of selling experience may in fact be more equipped to dialogue with a prospect than a salesperson with 20 years of experience—but we also found that, overall, *very few salespeople had a value statement that generated interest during first contact.* Certainly, those salespeople who had a high degree of success seemed to have a better chance at stumbling through with a rough value statement. They were good enough on their feet, so to speak, that they could deliver an average value statement and somehow create interest on the call. But most rookie salespeople didn't have a chance!

Construction of Value Statements

A powerful *value statement* creates the opportunity for a salesperson to instill immediate interest in the person with whom they're making contact. Knowing what to say can lead to an appointment and, in turn, yield more *net new* business.

Case Study

We were asked by a well-known organization to instruct their salespeople on the art of making contact with decision makers. This company had an excellent brand and a high-interest product. The company had two groups of salespeople. One group was made up of rookies (Group I) and the second group was more experienced (the customer relations team, or CRT). Both groups were responsible for driving net new business and reached out to corporations of all sizes. Their target contact was the CEO or one of the upper C-level executives who had P&L responsibility. At the time, the organization was reaching decision makers approximately 10 to 15 percent of the time when making cold prospecting calls. The sales manager said that the ability of the team to get an appointment once contact was made was estimated to be 20 percent. After delivering the SOAR formula, we began the live dialing segment of the program. Each salesperson was given the opportunity to *live* dial several times within his or her respective group in front of the SOAR instructor and team. Upon completion of the dialing, we recorded metrics illustrated in the following Figure 7-1. (Note: initially, Dialexis did not conduct in-depth value statement training because the client stated that their teams were competent in the area of delivering value statements.)

Contact rate before SOAR training: 15%	Contact rate after SOAR training: 83%
The appointment rate the sales manager believed they would get was: 20%	Actual appointment rate: 8%

Figure 7-1 *VS Chart Before and After Training*

Right away, it was apparent that the SOAR process was causing a significant improvement when it came to making *contact*. However, we discovered that the sales teams were less skilled at presenting a value statement as was indicated by their very low 8 percent appointment rate. The VP of sales (who stayed in the training), who had believed they would be excellent at value statements, was flabbergasted! He couldn't believe both teams were so bad at delivering a value statement. We suggested we conduct an extensive value statement training to provide the sales teams with improved value statements. During that time, we created multiple value statements and answers to potential objections a prospect would likely deliver. Value statements were created for contacting the CEO and other executive levels for both groups. We then moved forward and, now armed with value statements and answers to objections, began a three-month (12-week) measurement process. Figure 7-2 shows the results measured over that period:

For the Group I team, the results show a contact rate of 83 percent to decision makers or high influencers and a 12 percent appointment rate. The contact rate improved from 15 percent to 83 percent, while the appointment rate improved from 8 percent to 12 percent. The

SOAR running stats		100%	40%	60%	Contacts			88%			20–30%				
Group I team	Contact goal	Gross calls	N/A	Net calls	DM	HI	Total	In rate %	% of goal	Total appt.	Appt. %	Projected revenue	Closed revenue	% Closed
Sales rep 1	251	254	107	147	62	58	120	82%	48%	26	18%	$535,000	$36,650	7%
Sales rep 2	493	403	65	338	74	173	247	73%	50%	15	4%	$218,500	$43,500	20%
Sales rep 3	493	454	161	293	48	221	269	92%	55%	23	8%	$50,000	$16,500	33%
Sales rep 4	381	270	72	198	39	120	159	80%	42%	35	18%	$48,500	$18,500	38%
Sales rep 5	265	380	147	233	126	73	199	85%	75%	42	18%	$46,500	$22,000	47%
Sales rep 6	315	520	199	321	132	118	250	78%	79%	25	8%	$96,000	$8,600	9%
Sales rep 7	160	98	50	48	10	34	44	92%	28%	9	19%	$35,000	$2,500	7%
Sales rep 8	170	115	55	60	19	37	56	93%	33%	15	25%	$21,750	$6,710	31%
Sales rep 9	140	86	26	60	35	24	59	98%	42%	9	15%	$65,500	$0	0%
Sales rep 10	128	106	42	64	23	38	61	95%	48%	18	28%	$37,500	$27,500	73%
Sales rep 11	140	108	53	55	18	28	46	84%	33%	7	13%	$42,500	$27,500	65%
Total	2936	2794	977	1817	586	924	1510	83%	51%	224	12%	$1,196,750	$209,960	17.5%
Customer relations team														
Customer rep 1	580	441	175	266	208	58	266	100%	46%	97	36%			
Customer rep 2	620	516	221	295	183	91	274	93%	44%	97	33%			
Customer rep 3	620	556	250	306	160	133	293	96%	47%	77	25%			
Customer rep 4	320	145	83	62	35	27	62	100%	19%	29	47%			
Total	2140	1658	729	929	586	309	895	96%	42%	300	32%	n/a	n/a	n/a

Figure 7-2 *Detailed Performance Results Chart (Value Statement)*

50 percent jump for Group I in appointments, although not impressive, did make a significance difference in terms of producing more opportunities. For the more experienced customer relations team, the overall contact rate was 96 percent with an appointment rate of 32 percent.

It was apparent that, with less experience, Group I would need to further develop their value statements and objection handling going forward, and that they would have to produce a more refined delivery when giving value statements. The customer relations team, on the other hand, showed that experience matters: their contact rate went up to 96 percent on net new dials and their appointment rate grew to an impressive 32 percent. (Remember, these were ice cold calls.) (The customer relations team opted to not measure post-SOAR training, while the less experienced group's results were measured.)

The gross ROI for Group I was approximately 949.80 percent over the three-month measurement period considering their initial investment in SOAR.

What you say to a large target account versus a small account is dramatically different. Let's look at the list of baseline components we suggest you consider before you actually build your value statements. Here are two preparatory steps:

1. **List Your Value Add's**

   Corporate Value Add's (CVA).   *Corporate value adds* are those things that your organization has that other competitive organizations have. For example: the other organizations have an extended maintenance program and your firm has an extended maintenance program; they have cloud technology and your firm has cloud technology; they have on time delivery and your firm has on time delivery; they have engineering support and your firm has engineering support; and so on. Corporate value-adds are anything that keeps your organization at a parity with the competition. List those CVAs that you think are the most important your organization has.

Unique Marginal Differentiators (UMD). These are the differentiators your firm has that you believe the competition *does not* have. For example, your firm may have 24-hour guaranteed turnaround and the competition does not; your firm may have an inside design group, and the competition does not. UMDs are those things that your company possesses that the competitors simply don't have or can't compete with. They are very powerful when applied to a value statement. List any UMDs you have— that is, your differentiators.

Personal Values Add's (PVA). Just as your company may have key differentiators; *you* may have *personal* differentiators as well. Review what you bring to the table that the majority of your sales rep competitors do not: Perhaps you have an engineering degree or maybe you were a lean manufacturing consultant prior to your current position. Perhaps you were a specialist in a given field in the military. The point is, you get to evaluate what it is that *you* personally bring to the prospect that other competitors may not provide. Make a list of any differentiators you personally have. In some organizations there are few, if any, UMD's; there may be very little that sets them apart from the competition, so the only thing you can do is find what differentiates *you* from your competition. Ask a few people who know you well to give you authentic feedback about what key traits they see in you (responsible, honest, creative, intelligent, etc.) and develop a list. After you have that list, visit or call a few past or current clients and ask them what they think differentiates you from other salespeople. Explain to them that you are interested in knowing your strengths as a sales professional. Ask them what they like about your interaction with them and what they experienced as your most important differentiator. You might be surprised to learn about your PVA's. You may have heard the slogan, "people buy from people they like and trust." We tend to agree; clients typically buy from people they like and respect. So your personal value differentiators are most likely why clients may buy from you or continue to do business with you!

2. A Value Add Discovery Exercise

You will need a partner for this. On a piece of paper, write "I want an appointment" (since we assume the reason you are calling is to get an appointment). Then, on the right side of the paper, list the following words that your partner can ask you that you will have to defend (why anyone would want to have an appointment with you). List these words:

Why	**Where**
How	**When**
Who	**Proof**
What	

Hand the paper to your partner and have your partner begin asking the questions above. As you defend the words your partner is asking, you will soon begin to say things that are more compelling than the initial statement most salespeople make at the beginning of a call, such as, "I can help you save money."

Example of how the exercise will play out:

You: I want an appointment. (*this is your opening statement to your partner*)

Partner: WHY would someone want to meet with you? (*here's your first challenge*)

You: Because I can help them save money. (*typical salesperson response . . . how boring*)

Partner: HOW can you help me save money? (*you knew this was coming*)

You: Because we have done it many times. (*you had better be ready to defend!*)

Partner: WHO have you done it for? (*you better have the names!*)

You: The Smith Company, The Jones Company, and The Anderson Company. (*great job!*)

Partner: HOW did you help them save money? (*the questions are getting deeper*)

You: We introduced our initial CCE Process. (*now we're hearing something interesting*)

Partner: WHAT is CCE? (*can't use acronyms without explaining!*)

You: CCE is our Corporate Compliance Evaluation, which is an initial evaluation to determine if your company is in compliance with FCC regulations. The great thing is that we conduct this with no initial fee, and we are proud to say that we are the only organization offering this evaluation. (*now we're discovering something really interesting: a differentiator!*)

Partner: WHAT results have you found?

You: During our evaluations, we have found that 7 out of 10 companies were not in compliance and were therefore at risk for substantial penalties by the FCC. The good thing is that we were able to make appropriate corrections within 30 days of our initial free evaluation. (*good stuff!*)

Partner: Do you have PROOF of that statement? (*can't make statements without proof!*)

You: Absolutely! We have CCE results for every organization we have served. (*excellent!*) (*Remember, you will need approval from the organizations you have served before you release any confidential data.*)

The purpose of this exercise is to get you to think deeper relative to what you bring to your clients. Most salespeople begin their value statement on the telephone with some kind of generic remark about saving the client money. The fact is, there are many other statements you can create that are significantly more powerful as your opening value statement. When you do this exercise, you will discover that, as you go deeper and deeper and work harder at defending your statements, that the information becomes more valuable to the client.

Instead of saying something like:

"John, my name is Ed Lewis, and the reason I am calling is to talk to you about how my company can save you money."

You now can say something like:

"John, my name is Ed Lewis. I am with The ABC Company, and the reason I am calling is to introduce you to our CCE Compliance format that The Anderson Company, The Smith Company, and others have used." Or . . .

"John, my name is Ed Lewis. I am with The ABC Company, and we have recently found that 7 out of 10 organizations were out of FCC compliance. I wanted to take a moment to let you know how we brought them into compliance." Or . . .

"John, my name is Ed Lewis. I am with an organization that brings companies into FCC Compliance. Do you know if your company is in FCC compliance? When would you be open to a 15-minute conversation about learning more about FCC compliance and the benefits?"

You get the point, don't you? By doing this exercise you dig out the things that you can bring to the forefront of your initial value statement that might ordinarily go undiscovered.

Additional Value Statement Suggestions

Delivery of your value statement should take no more than 15 to 20 seconds—generally less. Most salespeople believe that a value statement cannot exceed 10 or 15 seconds. However, we know that having a value statement that takes as long as 20 to 30 seconds is possible based upon two things: first, how you deliver the value statement, and second, how relevant it is to the prospect's *corporate initiative* or *pain*. As a result, when you construct your value statement, keep it simple, and then learn how to say it so it has impact. You can't sound like you are reading a script. The delivery has to be very conversational and interesting to your listener. Remember, when making *net new* business development calls, the prospect isn't even connecting with what you are saying in the first few seconds, so you may need to slow down at the start.

You most likely will need several value statements. For example, the variables could be:

1. Adjust your value statement to the title of the person you are calling (CEO, CFO, CIO, Purchasing or the product line vertical you are representing, etc.)

2. Create a different value statement for an enterprise account as oppose to a transactional account.

   An enterprise account will respond best to a value statement that touches on the organization's corporate initiative, which, as we have said, you can find through researching the account prior to making contact.

3. For a transactional B2B account, you simply need an understanding of the "general pain" associated with their industry; your value statement should offer a solution.

When constructing your value statement, build it from your organization's or your personal *differentiator*; that is, your *unique marginal difference*. You may have several products, solutions, or services, but it is best to lead with the one that is the most powerful or unique. In the case of the enterprise account, lead with the product that best supports the corporate initiative of the organization you are calling. Why call and say what others say? Find something unique about you or your organization that you can put it into your value statement. This is your differentiator.

Once you develop your value statement in writing, see how many irrelevant words you can take out while still saying the same thing and having the same impact. Rewrite it until it is succinct.

Role-play your value statement over the telephone with a peer to see what feedback you get. Remember, it's often not just what you say, but how you say it. Practice, practice, practice. . .

Create several value statements to determine which is best. A client's response will tell you how relevant your value statement is.

Sample Value Statements

The following is a list of sample value statements that we share with salespeople working for Dialexis. Our sales personnel are not required to implement the following examples, but they do use them as a guide to constructing their own value statements. Since they know their prospecting targets, it is incumbent upon them to construct a value statement that best relates to the contact they are calling.

Value Statement Examples

"John, my name is [your name] and I am with an organization out of California that instructs salespeople how to drive *net new business. Do you have a moment to speak?*"

(We realize we are ending with a closed-ended question. However, we find it works for us.)

"John, my name is [your name], and I am with an organization out of California that instructs salespeople how to get *appointments* with decision makers. Is this an area of interest to you?"

"John, my name is [your name], and I am with an organization out of California that instructs salespeople how to make *contact* with decision makers. May I ask how important you feel this is to your selling process?"

"John, my name is [your name], and I'm with a company called Dialexis. I was just reading all the bad economic news in *The Wall Street Journal,* and I thought you might like a little good news! Our organization is introducing a new revenue-driving program that is currently utilized by many Fortune 500 companies, and I wanted to send you an overview of the program to see if you find it valuable for your sales team."

"John, my name is [your name], and I'm with an organization out of California called Dialexis. We are currently launching a new and very powerful revenue-driving program for sales, and I wanted to ask you a few questions to see if the program would be worth your evaluation. Do you have a quick minute?"

"John, my name is [your name], and I'm with an organization out of California called Dialexis. I know you are familiar with SPIN Selling, Strategic Selling, PSS, and similar sales programs, all of which teach salespeople what to do *once they get in* to a call. I thought you may be interested in a program that teaches salespeople *how to get in.*"

"Good morning, John, my name is [your name]. I am with a company called Dialexis, and we help salespeople develop effective mindset techniques. The reason I'm calling is to ask if you have any salespeople on your team that are not hitting their numbers who could use a mindset shift?"

"I am with a company that interacts with many large organizations' sales teams, and most recently with [name of organization]. The reason I'm calling is to ask if you would be interested in reviewing a *net new* revenue-driving program."

"Good morning, John, my name is [your name]. I am with a company called Dialexis, and we help salespeople develop effective demand generation techniques. The reason I'm calling you is to ask if you would be interested in an article we authored about how to get salespeople to drive *net new business*? I would be happy to send it to you, and I would appreciate your feedback."

"Good morning, John, my name is [your name]. I am doing what you most likely want your salespeople to do, and that is *prospecting*. The reason I am calling is because we just completed a demand generation program with (client name) during which we instructed their sales team how to drive net new business. Do you have a moment?"

Speaking to the EAP

"We are introducing a new revenue-driving program, and I wanted to ask you who you think I should submit the information to. *Generally, I speak to the president or SVP of sales.* Who do you think would have the most interest?"

When the EAP says *"Send it to me"* this is the talk-trac you could pursue:

"I would be happy to, [address the EAP by name]. May I ask how the process would go? For example, when do you think you would get it into the hands of [the CEO's name]? Is this something you think [the CEO] would have interest in?"

An additional EAP talk-trac for Dialexis salespeople:

"Are you Bill's executive assistant? [the EAP says yes] Excellent. My name is [your name], and you are the perfect one for me to reach. I am with a company out of California called Dialexis, and the reason I am calling is to invite Bill to an event. Do you keep his calendar? We are hosting a 20-minute webinar on [topic] with other executives during which we'll introduce a *net new* revenue driving program that has been field tested with (clients' names). The webinar will be held at [date and time]. This is simply an informative webinar, and Bill can preview it from his desk. Do you keep his calendar?"

The Lion and the Ring of Fire

We used to go to see the Ringling Brothers Circus when we were children. One act featured a lion that the "ringmaster" would induce to jump through a ring of fire. Back then we thought the reason that the lion responded and jumped through the ring of fire was that the ringmaster had a big whip that he would snap vigorously at the lion. We assumed the lion was afraid of the whip. Well, today we realize there was much more going on than simply the whip; animal trainers all over the world use a reward, usually food, to get animals to behave a certain way. The parallel here is that salespeople are much the same. Most show up to work every day because the trainer (boss) uses food (money) to get them to do something they may not even want to do.

The story of the lion has a wonderful application to value statement creation. As you review your CVAs, PVAs, and UMDs, you have the opportunity to decide what the "food" is that will cause your target prospect to want to meet with you, to jump through the ring of fire, so to speak. A lion jumps through a fire ring for raw meat, but not fresh fruit; there is a "right" kind of food that must be offered. Similarly, what is the "right" food (value statement) you need to use with your prospect? If you reach a target prospect and, after delivering your value statement, you haven't created interest, it may be time to change your value statement. The target prospect is essentially saying, "I'm not interested because your value statement isn't interesting enough"—that is, it's not the "right food."

Transactional and Major Account Value Statements

- **Transactional formula: P + D = VS** (Pain + Differentiator = Value Statement)

- **Major Account formula: R + CI + D = VS** (Research + Corporate Initiative + Differentiator = Value Statement)

The next step to creating your value statement is to determine what the motivator (the "right food") is for the smaller accounts vs. the large enterprise accounts. We look at the distinction this way:

Transactional Value Statements

Transactional selling focuses on more of a hit-and-run approach, making call after call. You seek an immediate opportunity and tend not to be focused on the value of building a long-term relationship.

You may even be able to close the sale over the telephone during the first call.

Structuring a value statement when dialing transactionally does not necessarily require pre-research; you simply may have to know one thing: the commonly understood pain of the industry you are calling. For example, in the commercial real estate industry, an office broker calling on accounts that have a lease on their office space will generally have many issues he or she can address on the initial call. However, the one issue that all tenants would want to resolve would be lowering their rent or restructuring their lease. Therefore, a commercial real estate broker may structure a value statement around a suggested "audit" to investigate the prospect's existing lease to see if there is any way to lower the tenant's current lease rate. Notice I said "audit"; that implies that the broker has a format or audit process to suggest to the prospect. In short, the audit process becomes the broker's differentiator. As a result, the broker can structure a value statement with the formula $P + D = VS$. In this case, the tenant's pain would be a high lease payment and the differentiator would be the broker's audit. Armed with these two key components, the broker can construct a compelling value statement.

In your case, all you have to do is understand the common pain the industry or target that you are calling has, then be sure you have a solution to that pain (which could be your differentiator) and create your value statement from that beginning point. In summary, with a transactional selling model you always look for the "commonly understood pain" clients have in their respective industry. You should know what that pain is if you are familiar with the industry in which you sell. Again, in this case the commercial broker knows that one common pain or interest point in the office market is "rent reduction."

Major Account Value Statements

In major account selling, you may be seeking to contact larger enterprise accounts and build long-term relationships. These accounts can be complex with multiple locations throughout the country or, for that matter, throughout the world. With these enterprise accounts, you will not be making a sequence of quick dials one after another, but instead calling with a strategic approach armed with extensive pre-research.

Structuring your value statement for the more complex account is much different from the quick transactional approach. The formula we suggest with these enterprise accounts is R + CI + D = VS (Research + Corporate Initiative + Differentiator = Value Statement). You would begin by searching online or finding any segment of information that reveals key facts about the account. In this case, you would be looking for the organization's *corporate initiative*. We are not talking about the company's mission statement; we're speaking about the organization's current initiative or initiatives. When looking online, you can find an organization's corporate initiative in the President's Letter to the Shareholders or in their Annual Report, or sometimes in the Media portion of their website.

Here is an example of a corporate initiative of a Dialexis client, Jones Lang LaSalle, a world-class commercial real estate firm. We discovered this initiative on their website under their Proxy Statement–Annual Meeting Shareholder Report. The stated JLL corporate initiative was called G5. It is the company's five global strategic priorities, and they are listed as:

- **G1:** Build our leading and local and regional market positions;
- **G2:** Grow our leading positions in the corporate solutions business;
- **G3:** Capture the leading share of global capital flows for investment sales;
- **G4:** Strengthen LaSalle Capital Investment, Capital Managements leadership position; and
- **G5:** Differentiate our business by connecting across the firm and with clients.

What we have found when going through this process is that it often is inspiring to learn what a company stands for. It can create a new energy for making the initial call.

So, when you decide what size organizations your demand creation activity will be targeting, remember to take the following into consideration:

- Small B2B companies: If you are targeting smaller firms, we suggest you use the formula P + D = VS (Pain + Differentiator = Value Statement) for developing your value statement.

- Enterprise target accounts: The formula for creating a value statement for larger accounts is R + CI + D + V (Research + Corporate Initiative + Differentiator = Value Statement.

Value Statement Delivery

As we mentioned, the *delivery* of a value statement is as important as the value statement itself. The way you hesitate, change your tone, emphasize your words, and so on are critical when attempting to get the most out of presenting your value statement to a prospect. Just as actors learn to say their lines in a certain way, you need to adapt the way you deliver your value statement. Our recommendation is to create what you think is a compelling value statement, then test the impact of your value statement and your delivery with your sales manager. Tell your sales manager you want to practice this over the telephone rather than in person, because that is most likely the way you will be delivering it. Ask for feedback and be open to it. Another option is practice with a friend, a salesperson, or your spouse. Practice and feedback are the keys to honing your value statement and particularly your delivery of it.

Generic Value Statement (SOAR)

When we teach SOAR, we offer the sales attendees a generic value statement because most of them don't have a prepared value statement. The one we provide is, "Jan, my name is John Smith, and the reason I'm calling is that, during this time of great change, I thought this would be a good time to . . ." This is where you can add why you are calling from a value statement perspective. You can also ask when is a good time to *meet* or a good time to *discuss* or a good time to introduce your topic.

In the generic value statement, change implies many things, such as market conditions, the economy, new initiatives, mergers, technology advances, new contracts, moving/relocating, and so forth. When you refer to *change,* you are not suggesting you know what change the organization is personally going through, but simply that *change in general* is a given with all organizations. So if the person you are speaking to says, "how do you know what kind of change we are going through?" you simply reply, "I don't specifically, I am only saying that organizations are experiencing a great deal of *change* in general. As a result, the reason I am calling is . . ." Every company is going through some sort of change, so speaking to the prospect with a "change" statement often opens up communication.

By the way, we experienced a salesperson in the live dialing segment of SOAR who would call and simply say, "the reason I am calling is to set an appointment with you?" She frequently received a reply of, "why do you want to meet?" or "who are you?" or something similar She would then state why she was calling, delivering a more conversational value statement. (Obviously, this would be after you made your initial statement of introduction.)

You will need to practice delivering your value statement until whoever you practiced it with says it sounds natural. As we said, have others listen and give feedback as to how natural you sound. Again, you don't want to sound like you are reading from a script.

Summary

A value statement and a value proposition are different. SOAR is primarily involved with value statements.

Key points about the critical value statement:

- Use the formula CP + D = VS for transactional targets and R + CI + D = VS for enterprise targets.

- Having a value statement alone may not yield success on a call; the way the value statement is delivered is key.
- Practice delivering your value statement with your sales manager.
- Discover how your differentiator "connects" to the target client's corporate initiative.
- Value statements should not be read; list your value offerings and your differentiators on a piece of paper so you can simply look at them when delivering your value statement. By doing this you will avoid reading and sound more natural as you "pick off" the key points you have listed.

8

UNDERSTANDING THE BEHAVIOR OF YOUR PROSPECTS AND CLIENTS

DiSC®: The Art of Reading People

Dialexis uses Inscape Publishing's DiSC® behavioral assessments in SOAR training. DiSC is an invaluable tool for helping salespeople understand their prospects or even their existing clients or customers. DiSC increases your awareness of your client's behavioral style, providing you with a framework for generating a successful call result. Simply put, DiSC is about understanding how to best communicate with your clients or prospective clients.

People see the world in different ways and are motivated by different things. DiSC breaks behavior styles into four categories: "D" Dominant, "i" Influencer, "S" Steady, and "C" Conscientious. Each type appreciates communication that is similar to their style. If you're dealing with a Dominant style, you will be expected to get to the point quickly, whereas with the Conscientious style, you may have to put in more time and provide more information to let that person process what you are saying. Dominant styles like the big picture overview and make most decisions with their "gut"; a person with a Conscientious behavioral style makes decisions by knowing the facts and weighs the pros and cons to come to a thoughtful decision or choice.

Your ability to adapt to your clients' style is key. This is true because you are trying to *connect* with the people you are contacting. Connecting with them improves the odds of getting an appointment. DiSC is a critical part of building rapport and helps you to be adaptive in your sales approach so you can be successful with all behavioral styles. Throughout this book, you will see that SOAR and its DiSC component represents a powerful tool when put into determined hands.

The following represents a crash course in DiSC for understanding prospects' behavioral style. The most important component is that you match *your* style to *their* style when prospecting. The interesting thing is that, as you become more familiar with DiSC, you will be able to determine the style of the person you are speaking to on the telephone more and more quickly.

The Four Behavior Groups
and What They Mean

"D" Dominant Style.   Fast; likes options, wants results. People who fall into the Dominant category often answer on speakerphone. They sound very strong and confident, yet don't talk much; they get to the point. You will know you have a "D" on your call because she will tell it like she sees it. She may directly challenge what you're saying. You may feel intimidated; people with a "D" style can sometimes come at you with their confidence. Be ready and get to the point. Explain how your offer can generate results quickly. "Ds" won't like lengthy value statements or rambling. People with a "D" style like power and challenge.

"i" Influencer Style.   Social, friendly, relates to energy. You will know when you have an "i" on the telephone because this type is extremely friendly. You will get a sense he is there to support you. So, smile as you speak into the phone. Be friendly and convey energy. Use his name. People with the "i" style want and love being included, so don't hesitate to ask for help or pose questions. They want to talk with you. Be sure to let them speak. They will love hearing about some of your other high-profile clients because they like being part of the "in crowd."

"S" Steady Style.   Steady, calming, pleasant team player; likes process. On the phone you will feel this style's gentle way. People with an "S" style are agreeable and patient. They are composed. They don't necessarily connect with the energy of a "D" or "i". When speaking with people who have the "S" style, match your energy level with theirs, present yourself in a balanced manner, breathe, and take time between sharing your thoughts. Soften your voice and slow down; take an easy approach. Be sure to use their name. A side note: people with the "S" style have had friends since kindergarten, so don't think you will be their "friend" instantly. Maybe you can be an acquaintance right away, but being a friend will take time.

"C" Conscientious Style.   Very cautious and skeptical; wants proof and wants details. You will recognize this type on the call because she may not give you much. She may even answer the phone in a very formal manner. "C" types will listen, but they may challenge you on your offer and they might not feel warm. Do not use your big personality. Drop the energy, slow down, and get to the point with clarity while offering details. Warning: know the answers to their questions and be prepared to back your answers up or tell them you will get back to them with the appropriate answer. They will respect that: "C" styles like people with extreme product knowledge.

Adapting Your Style to Your Prospects' or Clients' Styles

In order to be proficient with DiSC you will need to study the DiSC information in detail. Becoming excellent at identifying a prospect's style on the telephone also requires you to be extremely present. You can't just dial away without thinking; you have to really listen in order know the style of the person you are speaking to. Here are some helpful tips:

How the "D" Sounds on a Call.   A "D" may answer the telephone with strength in his voice. You will hear his confidence. He may abruptly answer, "Yes?" or, "This is Don." Once he answers and you deliver your value statement, he will either immediately tell you what he thinks in a direct way or he will get right to asking you a question—and he may ask that question in a challenging way. You will feel a "D's" directness and you may be intimidated, so be ready. You will have to be prepared because people with a "D" style are hard to keep on a call unless you have something very compelling to say. Don't expect a friendly voice or compassionate response to your value statement. Once they say no, you may have only one shot to restate your value statement; after that they can become aggressive or disengage. Again, they like power and confidence; they are driven by their ego and are comfortable with other powerful people. However, always give them choices because they like being in control.

How the i Sounds on a Call.   Here is the good news: the "i" will sound friendly. But don't let that fool you! Just because an "i" sounds friendly doesn't mean she is interested. Encouragement is not an indicator of interest; it's an indicator that you are speaking with a high "i". Remember, an "i" won't want to hurt your feelings or be perceived as rude, so, rather than say "no," or "I'm not interested," they may encourage you by requesting that you send them something, even though they may have very little interest. It will be important for you to qualify the "send me something" (SMS) response in such a way that you give the "i" a chance to be candid. The bottom line is that "i" styles want to be liked, and they don't want to disappoint you. Also be aware that, just because the "i" is friendly and the sound of her voice may encourage you to keep attempting to generate interest, ultimately, if you push too hard, an "i" may bite!

How the S Sounds on a Call.   Remember that the "S" is steady and smooth. Not a lot of emotion here; just a matter-of-fact, gentle, and pleasant way. People with an "S" style will sound polite and possibly timid. You will hear efficient language. Like an "i," they won't want to offend, but they will tell you if they are interested or not if you give them time to speak. "S" styles are great listeners, and it's valuable to give them a "space" in the conversation to deliver their thoughts. If they request something to be sent, they may be more interested than not, but it's going to require you to *qualify* their request, just as you would do with an "i."

How the "C" Sounds on a Call.   With the "C," you shouldn't expect emotion, friendliness, or much dialogue; they are fairly formal (they sometimes address themselves by their formal name: Cynthia not Cindy, Deborah not Debbie, or David not Dave). They may respond with questions and challenges that are not relevant to your value statement, such as, "how did you get my number?"

Again, as is the case with the "D," do not expect to hear a smile on the phone. You may even feel as though they hung up: they will listen so intently that they won't say much. Know that their close listening may not be because they are trying to understand you so much as determine how they can dispute your statements.

An important note: Not everyone you call is going to be just one style. Many people you prospect will have two or more behavior styles, but you can usually "hear" their primary behavioral style when they answer the telephone. For example, you may get a "high D" on a call that also has an "i" as a secondary style. If this is the case, how he behaves on one call may not be how he behaves on a subsequent call, so be careful not to *box him in.* Again, adapt. Ask him "telling" questions. Here is a great question to help you identify the "primary" behavioral style. If you were asking someone about sending him something or making a presentation you would say:

"How would you like me to present this information: high-level or detailed?"

- If the answer is "high-level," you are speaking to a "D."

- If the answer is "detailed," you are most likely speaking to a "C".

- If the prospect answers with, "Either way. Where should we meet?" that is most likely an "i."

- If the prospect answers in a slow, calm tone, "I would like to have more information in order to consider the possibility of a future meeting, is that alright?" he may be an "S."

Motivating and Connecting

The best way to motivate or connect to people is to be like they are— to mirror them. During your calls, you will essentially need to listen very carefully to what you are hearing in the contact's voice and adapt to that style. You will most likely have to abandon your natural style to do this because the worst thing any salesperson can do is to continue to use his own behavior style with a person of another style. For example, if you are an "i" and you are speaking to a "C," you are going to have to adapt quickly. If you believe you have a "C" on the telephone and you continue to use your "i" style, it's going to be a disaster: the energy an "i" exudes is generally the complete opposite of how a "C" feels. As a rule of thumb, until you understand DiSC more thoroughly, simply match the other person's behavior. That means tone, speed of speaking, sense of humor (or lack thereof), energy level, and so forth. Also find out what *your* style is and then delve deeper to get a sense of your strengths and weaknesses so you can connect well with others.

Summary

Key points about understanding the behavior of your prospects and clients:

- DiSC is a quadrant behavioral model based on the work of Dr. William Moulton Marston (1893–1947). DiSC examines the behavior of individuals in their environment or in a specific situation. It therefore focuses on the styles and preferences of such behavior.
- Learning to *connect* with your prospect or client and to "mirror" the person on a net new call is vital to making a successful net new contact. DiSC supports that process.
- Understanding what motivates different behavioral styles is powerful for any salesperson. Learning the DiSC language provides salespeople with an advantage.
- You must adapt to the person you are making contact with—not the other way around.
- Using only one DiSC style of "connecting" with each new contact you make can lead to an ineffective call. It's imperative you adapt—begin by knowing your DiSC style.
- Study other styles so you understand what motivates different styles.

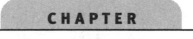

CHAPTER

HANDLING OBJECTIONS

Product Knowledge, Market Knowledge, Competitor Knowledge, and Client Knowledge

One of the most useful tips we can give you when it comes to handling objections is that *you have to know what you are talking about.* Whether you are a new salesperson or an experienced salesperson, and whether you're part of a new company or representing a new product, dealing with objections can sometimes be daunting. Some of your best tools will be being skilled at product knowledge and objection handling, and, as we said earlier, most corporate training departments are doing an amazing job at training product knowledge, competitive knowledge, and base objection handling.

Very simply . . . you have to know your stuff! In the course of providing SOAR training, as we traveled extensively and engaged with multiple Fortune-500 companies, there wasn't one that didn't stress the importance of product knowledge to their sales teams. But even if the company is doing a competent job of getting you up to speed on what you will be selling, there is still much to know. Senior salespeople that have been in the field for a long time with the same organization may have the best information when it comes to *objection handling* because they are so practiced at it.

Here are a few tips we can offer to get you up to speed. These apply whether you are rookie or an experienced salesperson.

1. **Take extensive notes during training.** If you are new with the organization, you will be attending some kind of training. That training will most likely be focused on product knowledge and, in many cases, objection handling, so don't lose focus. You really need to use discipline and solid note-taking during your sessions with your corporate trainers, even if you are an experienced salesperson. When we were in the initial training sessions in the commercial real estate industry, we really didn't know what to pay attention to and it was sometimes challenging to stay focused—and we are very experienced salespeople. We did take extensive notes, however, despite not knowing what was critical and what may not have been.

2. **Keep your training notes close at hand.** Whatever you learn, whatever you have been told and recorded in writing, whatever the company has handed out to you as collateral, you want to keep it close at hand. You may think that much of what was given during training is irrelevant, but, eventually, you will find it's of immense value when you get to the field. If you are a rookie, this isn't a college class you attend where you can learn the material, pass the test, and then forget what you learned. If you are an experienced salesperson, you certainly know the importance of product knowledge and objection handling. Remember to be humble. Some of the best salespeople we've had the good fortune to know have somehow remained humble. Arrogance shuts the door to learning.

The information you are exposed to relative to product knowledge and objection handling can sometimes make the difference between winning and losing a key sale. Save it and read it often; make it your "go-to." Get to know it backward and forward. Some day, on a prospecting call or during a meeting, you know you are going to be tested. How you handle questions and objections may make the difference between taking you to the top 20 percent or keeping you in the 80 percent, even if you have previous sales experience. It will also be the differentiator between serving your customer or not, staying in your career or not, taking your dream vacation or not, helping someone in your family or not, giving back to your community or not, buying your first home or not . . . it's that important.

3. **Talk to the pros.** We have found that the salespeople that are successful in the organization and that ranked in the top 20 percent or greater know product knowledge and objection handling the best. So do many of the support staff, like researchers, technicians, IT, and so on. Find out who the top people are in your company and reach out to them. If you are a rookie, you simply call them or sit with them and say something like, "John, do you have a minute to talk? I am trying to sharpen my ability to handle objections, and knowing that you are more experienced and

considered a top rep, I would appreciate some coaching. Could I take you to lunch or meet you after hours for a few minutes to help me understand how you would handle objections?" Then ask a few well-thought-out questions, including, "What would you say are the three top objections that I can expect to hear on my prospecting calls, and how would you answer them?"

If you do this with a handful of top salespeople in your company, you will garner an amazing list of answers to tough objections while at the same time developing your product knowledge. Once you have done that, take the same approach with your sales manager. In the end, you will have saved yourself a lot of frustration trying to find the right answers to difficult objections. You will simply have to memorize the answers they give you and understand *why* they are applicable to the objection.

In order to handle objections well, you will also need to know as much as possible about your industry, your competitors, and your prospect so you can drive net new business. This is particularly true if the company you are prospecting is a high value target. Here are a few things to consider:

Your Industry.   Today, prospects are expecting extensive knowledge from salespeople and they will know quickly if you are product- and industry-savvy in the first few moments of dialogue with you. Salespeople can no longer fake knowledge and then expect a prospect to buy in. You have to know comparables, warranties, price factors, shipping, and a myriad of other components. If you are new to sales and have not learned what you need to, you won't be able to "get by" by flying by the seat of your pants or "winging it." Today, you must be an advisor and a trusted and respected resource. Your prospecting success will hinge greatly on your integrity and competency. You've *gotta be good*; you have to protect the best interests of your new clients, your organization, and your own personal reputation. You have to care more about providing a sound result than just your commission.

Your Competition.   You should know who you compete with. This includes not only the organizations that represent your greatest competition, but, in many cases, who you are personally selling against. Senior salespeople that are in a market long enough know who they compete with on a "salesperson-to-salesperson" level, not just the company they are lined up against. The pros often know the strength and weaknesses of those with whom they personally compete. For example, in commercial real estate, it was critical that we knew who the brokers were that we were competing against, as well as their approach and style. How could we win if we didn't know who or what we were up against? The best brokers knew it all.

Your Prospect.   Recall that in Chapter 6 we discussed the importance of pre-research when attempting to reach larger corporations or those you would consider enterprise prospects. The pre-research information you are seeking, as mentioned earlier, is the organization's corporate initiative. You will find the president's corporate initiative stated in the "Message from the President" on their website. Additionally, you can also gather a great deal of information on the organization's site relative to product offering, their differentiator, executive bios, and so forth. The last thing you want to do when implementing the SOAR formula is deliver a strong value statement relative to the client's corporate initiative and then crash and burn because you aren't prepared to answer the question, "what do you know about our company?" Do your research.

Objections and Listening: How They Go Hand in Hand

As mentioned earlier, in order to be as prepared as possible for handling objections, you obviously have to know what the objections are likely to be. However, without keyword listening as described in

Chapter 5, you could miss the *true* objection. For example, look at the following objections and consider what opportunity may have been missed by not picking up the *keyword*.

Objection: We're working with another vendor, but I appreciate your call.

Nonlistening response: When would be a better time to get back to you? (*or the salesperson begins to sell, sell, sell!*)

Listening response: John, when you say you are 'working with,' are you in a contract agreement? Can you help me understand what "working with" means?

That is just one response; there are numerous. The important thing is that the platform for a better response to the objection is launched from the keyword "working with." The salesperson should have heard the keyword so she can define what "working with" means. Is the client under a formal agreement? Have they actually started the relationship? Are they working with the client in all areas of their business? How long have they been working with the client, or what is the commitment period? Essentially, what does "working with" mean?

Here is another example:

Objection: Right now we are on a spending freeze, so you may want to give us a call next year.

Nonlistening response: I understand. In the meantime, may I send you something as an introduction to our organization, and then I will reach out to you next year?

Listening response: John, when you say "right now" and "next year," are you on a calendar year?

The point is, you have to hear the keywords "right now" and "next year." What if the prospect you are calling is on a *fiscal year*, not a *calendar year*, and their year is over in 30 days! You may be thinking in terms of a calendar year, and if it's only June you may not call the prospect back for five or six months! By this time, one of your competitors with better listening skills has already captured the deal. Learning to handle objections with keyword listening is a marriage made in heaven. To find the opportunity, you will not only have to learn counters to objections, but "listen" carefully for the revealing keywords.

Bundling: The Art of Getting All the Objections Using Keyword Listening

Salespeople are sometimes so eager to answer objections that they hear the first objection and hit the bait like a fish and start selling. By the time the prospect listens and responds to the salesperson's counter, time is up. The salesperson leaves, believing he knows the "real" reason why the target wasn't interested. What if the salesperson were to say, "John, may I ask *why* you are not interested?" Things could have gone this way:

Salesperson: May I ask why you are not interested?

Prospect: We are aware of your product and feel your pricing is too high.

Salesperson: Can you share with me what else keeps you from being interested?

Prospect: As we understand it, in order to get lower pricing from you, we have to purchase in larger quantities. Being a smaller company, that just doesn't work for us.

Salesperson: Is there anything else?

Prospect: The only other thing is the fact that I am retiring in 30 days, so my replacement will be making all purchasing decisions once the change happens.

We realize that this interchange between the salesperson and prospect is made up and may not be perfectly scripted as you think it may actually happen but the scripting is only to set an example of the power of *bundling*. Bundling is taking all of the client comments or objections and collecting them without any response from you. Salespeople often tend to hear one objection, and off they go. Just think how much would have been missed if the salesperson were to have stopped on the first objection and settled! By asking and bundling objections, the salesperson in this case discovered:

1. The prospect wasn't interested.

2. Pricing was too high.

3. The client feels they are too small to receive deeper discounting.

4. The prospect is going to retire in 30 days.

An entirely new series of questions become possible by listening, being patient and bundling . . . *then* solving. Why solve when you hear the first objection when oftentimes you may have the opportunity to "get it all" by keyword listening and asking more questions? Remember to *bundle before you solve.*

Certainly, you may not always have the opportunity to bundle on objections, but you can certainly take a shot at it, and if you can't get all the objections, as least you made the attempt and probably got more than you would have. Keyword listening and bundling are great partners when responding to objections!

Summary

Dialexis has learned from making live net new dials during the SOAR trainings that very senior salespeople are equipped with fairly solid objection-handling knowledge. However, newer salespeople are significantly unprepared to handle multiple or continuous objections. Be prepared with the typical objections.

Key points about handling objections:

- Handling objections requires more than simply product knowledge. Market knowledge, competitor product knowledge, and target client product knowledge are also imperative.
- Handling objections requires intense listening.
- Objections shouldn't promote "selling" immediately following the objection.
- Caring about the client's best interest is hearing the objection.
- Asking senior salespeople and those with superior product knowledge within your firm what the most common objections are and what the best responses would be can dramatically speed up your objection handling execution.
- You cannot be considered a trusted advisor or respected consultant for your firm without superior product knowledge across all areas. Clients expect a professional salesperson to guide them.
- Ask questions about the objection so you know what is generating the objection. Remember to "bundle" objections: get everything out on the table before you solve.
- Test your ability to handle multiple objections a client may have by role-playing with your sales manager or the technical department of your firm.

CHAPTER

10

DEALING WITH THE "SEND ME SOMETHING" REQUEST

Creating a SMS File:
Make Your Time Matter

When you are in the process of driving new business, you will ulti-mately be receiving "send me something" requests frequently. This is just what happens to salespeople when calling on new prospects. If you are anything like most salespeople, you hate to do paperwork, so the last thing you want to do is put together a SMS package or e-mail every time a prospect says, "send me something."

Here is what we do (we are no different than you when it comes to disliking paperwork!). We have prepared a SMS file on our computer for nearly every SMS request we can imagine. We have video clips, one-page documents, two-page documents, testi-monials, articles, product outlines, contracts, and so forth, all pre-prepared. When a prospect requests a SMS, we simply go to our SMS file on the topic requested and send the appropriate material via e-mail (because we work all over the world). It takes only a few seconds, a minute at most. If you are working a local market, you will learn later in this chapter how to shift an SMS response into an appointment.

In putting together our pre-prepared SMS file, we also consider the person we are sending the information to. There will certainly be times when the prospect requests something that's not in your file, which requires you to "custom create" an appropriate SMS. Creating a custom response is much easier because you can often cut and paste from your existing SMS file. If nothing in your SMS file fits, then, of course, you have to build a new SMS response, but you will have eliminated a great deal of time if you have prepared your SMS responses in advance.

You may be asking yourself, "How am I supposed to know what to prepare in my SMS file if I don't know what the prospect is going to request?" If you are product-knowledge competent and have spent enough discovery time researching what the most common objec-tives will be, you will have a pretty good idea what should go into your SMS file.

You may say, "But I'm busy. How am I supposed to find time to create a master SMS file?" The answer is simple: find the time. Create your response file on the weekends, at night, or by going in very early in the morning. The bottom line is that it's worth spending the time on. In the end, you will have saved yourself more time than what it will take to create your SMS file. And, as the saying goes, time kills all deals, so the more prepared you are the more responsive you will be in sending the SMS requests.

SMS and Corporate Initiatives

When you decide to act on a SMS request, you can't just send anything. Your SMS must be powerful and connect to the prospect's *pain* or *corporate initiative* just as your value statement should. (You may want to go back to Chapter 7 and review content on value statements.) With smaller companies who may not post a corporate initiative on their website, you may be able to make an assumption, considering their industry and the general economy and how their industry is doing.

When the client says, "send me something," they are most likely going to be responding to something you said when you made the call if the SMS is authentic. The important thing to remember is when you connect your product offerings to the client's *pain or corporate initiative* or both is very powerful. You may say that you mentioned the corporate initiative when you gave your value statement, and that may be true, but by the time the SMS gets to the client, it's all just a blur . . . so connect the client's corporate initiative to your SMS once again. Once you send something, that SMS is now your representative. Make it good, tell them why this will support the client and what they are trying to accomplish.

Remember what we said in Chapter 7: match your SMS to the client's DiSC style. A D style will not want to read a five-page SMS; you are lucky if they read a half of a page! So make it bullet points and more of an executive summary. If you have been talking to a C style, you will want to send details and "proof," if you have it. They need facts to even consider what you are proposing. If you are sending something to an i style or S style, add something personal to the SMS. The i styles like to know who has been a customer, especially if they are high profile clients, and the S styles like to know you have long-standing clients.

Qualifying Your SMS Request: Is It a Lead or Not?

Every time we ask salespeople what "send me something" means, they reply, "they are just trying to get you off the phone," or "it's a brush-off," or "they don't want to talk to you," and so on. It's almost always a negative interpretation. When we ask them how they know, then the thought occurs to them that maybe they don't really know. They realize that they should have asked. The opportunity most salespeople miss is *not asking*. Instead, they just send something. It's often a waste of time and ultimately leads to a pipeline of low production. We have seen many salespeople keep a list of all the "send me somethings" they accumulate, assuming the requests will lead to opportunities and ultimately a deal. In the end, they may miss quota or worst yet not get a needed commission because the majority of the SMS requests were never real in the first place.

Since we find that most salespeople will just send something and get off the call, it's unusual for a salesperson to push deeper into qualifying the SMS request. Going deeper to qualify interest can be uncomfortable for some salespeople since it could be met with resistance. However, we believe resistance may be a sign the prospect is not really interested *despite* the fact he or she asked for something to be sent! If the prospect becomes annoyed, he or she actually may really *not* want something. So, isn't it better to know if the SMS is an authentic request and there is sincere interest? Of course, it's all an assumption on our part, until we qualify, but if prospective clients seem put off by a few questions, it's been our experience they really aren't interested. This is what we've seen over years of SMS requests.

Certainly, as you question to qualify the SMS, you would do so in a professional manner. Don't assume prospects are not interested; your objective is to qualify if they are interested and the manner in which they want you provide that information.

The point is that you don't want to become a "send me something" salesperson. If the prospect gets annoyed at deeper qualifying, you know you could lose the prospect and that it's possible the prospect actually was interested. But take that chance, because you can't afford to keep sending things assuming you're making progress when you aren't!

In the end, it's up to you if you want to qualify deeper. You may have your own unique way of responding to a SMS request; we have five responses we've found successful in terms of qualifying SMS interest. In each subsequent step, it is our intent to move closer to determining if the client's SMS request is authentic. There is no certainty you will find the underlying intention of the SMS request by executing the following steps; however, it's what we do in SOAR and it usually works quite well.

Response #1: "John, I would be happy to send something. What is your e-mail? I'll send something immediately. However, so that I send you the *right* information, may I ask a few questions? It will just take a few seconds."

This is a beginning qualifier. If prospects are interested, we think they will be open to a few questions. If they are *not* open to a few quick questions, then we believe you can begin to assume the SMS request interest level is not very strong or they may not actually be interested.

Response #2: "John, I would be happy to send something. However, the odds are that you are going to have a few questions once you receive the information, so why don't we simply set a time so that I can review the information with you?"

Again, this is to support them in understanding the materials you are sending. This can be a phone appointment or an in-person appointment—you gauge the receptiveness of your prospect.

Response #3: "John, often when I send things, I find sometimes they don't get looked at. Do you think you will have time to review what I send?"

This reply always creates discussion in our training sessions. Some salespeople feel it's too direct or they just are uncomfortable delivering this statement. Here is the logic: isn't it true that sometimes you send something and then discover the client didn't keep it or look at it at all? So, why not ask the SMS requester if he or she will take time to read what you send? It's a way of qualifying the SMS request. You can use your own style when delivering it so it fits your personality. If the prospect begins to show signs of impatience, then you may start to wonder if this is a legitimate SMS request.

Response #4: "Let's assume you like what you see. Would you then be open to setting an appointment?"

If the prospect says, "I don't know, I have to look at it first," then you can simply say, "I understand, I'm just saying that, presuming you like it, would you be open to setting an appointment?" If prospects then say yes, you can request they pencil in a date and time now because you believe they are going to like it. If prospects show frustration, then once again you can begin to assume you are getting to the truth, which may be that they really don't want you to send something. I know what you are thinking: why make someone angry, why take the risk? We don't feel we are taking a risk when we deliver those words, to us we are just *qualifying* the SMS. When clients say "send me something," most salespeople just do it. We qualify the request, *then* do it.

Response #5: "May I ask what one thing made you interested to learn more?"

This is a great way to open up the dialogue. Again, if prospects don't have time to expand, ask them what type of information they would like to see. If they don't have time to answer that question, ask for a follow-up call so you can get some preliminary information in order to provide them with the material that would best serve them. The goal is to be of service and to qualify if the SMS is real.

Converting Your SMS Request to an Appointment Using Response #6

Before we tell you about Response #6, let's explain how it came into being. Over the years, as SOAR was being created, we would constantly run into the "send me something" request. As a result, we developed a six-step process for qualifying the SMS. All the qualifying suggestions seemed to work pretty well, but #6 was one that seemed to *really* deliver results, so we took it off the list and made it its own category. We simply called it "Number Six." So, what was originally a six-step process for qualifying the SMS request now became a five-step process. Here is how Response #6 works as a stand-alone when the client says, "send me something:"

Response #6 "John [use his name], let me ask you this: would you mind if I dropped off the information at the receptionist's desk?"

(Pause for an answer. If you get an affirmative reply, then continue.)

"When I come by, would it be OK if I called you from the lobby so we can put a face to a voice? We can then talk more when you're ready."

(Wait for response. If given the go-ahead, go on.)

"When are you generally there?"

(Armed with this information, then continue.)

"So, if I came by on [date] at [time], would this work?"

This is a very powerful tool when you sell in a local market. You know what we are betting on, right? You know that by dropping it off at the receptionist's desk there is no threat; by suggesting a call from the lobby and simply putting a face to a voice you are betting they will come out to *just meet* and once they *see you* they may say, "why don't you come in?" Of course, it's a bit of a long shot, but during the SOAR Live training we execute #6, often with great success!

Summary

Salespeople frequently interpret the request to "send me something" as "not interested."

Key points about dealing with the "send me something" request:

- SMS is not always a no; it is often an authentic request due to interest. Knowing the difference requires qualifying the statement.
- Prepare a SMS file in your computer so that you have all the possible responses ready in the event you must reply via e-mail. Take the time to create a SMS file (generic yet specific if you are in vertical markets).
- If appropriate to your market, use a #6 response to create a face-to-face meeting.
- If you do send something, make sure it is compelling to the client's pain or corporate initiative.
- If you are using e-mail, customize your e-mail to reflect your conversation. Make it relevant and personal.

LEAVING A MOM (MESSAGE OF MYSTERY) WHEN YOU ARE OUT OF CONTACT OPTIONS

Getting Up to 85 Percent Call Back from Leaving a Message

As you learn the SOAR formula for making contact, you will find there is some room for leaving a message . . . *some* room. SOAR suggests that you get clear about making contact before you actually dial; that is, get your intention locked in to *make contact*. When you get into the mindset that you may not make contact, then you won't. It then becomes easy to slide into leaving a message, and soon enough you find yourself consistently leaving messages, especially when you are armed with a powerful message of mystery (MOM).

SOAR is about "making contact," not leaving messages. There is, however, a powerful strategy for leaving a message *when all else fails*, but it should be infrequent. If you understand that the formula SOAR provides allows you to make contact up to 90 percent of the time with every net dial, then message leaving is only 10 percent at best . . . not the other way around!

A True Story About Leaving a MOM

A few months ago, we were in San Francisco, California, training a group of top sales executives. Although they had hundreds of connections and credibility, they wanted to increase their "net new" clients, so they were utilizing SOAR as their method for reaching new logos. During the training, one of the attendees said, "Hey, I've got to tell you that I am using the MOM technique and it is amazing. I wouldn't have been able to have reach some of my desired targets without this process. . . . As great as SOAR is, the MOM is incredible!" Although he said he used the MOM technique sparingly, he mentioned that on the very difficult calls it worked wonders. There are cases where technology may prevent the SOAR process from working, so a MOM may be one of your last alternatives. Remember: *the goal is net new business while making fewer dials.*

When you are dialing, it is important to stay on the call using the SOAR techniques until you have made at least four attempts to talk to a decision maker or a high influencer on the same call without hanging up (if the company is large enough to attempt four contacts). If all four attempts to negotiate reaching a decision maker or high influencer fail, then we suggest leaving a MOM.

What we do *not* recommend is leaving a MOM when you have reached voice mail without having made several attempts to contact the person on the *first* call. Again, reaching voice mail on your initial call is a completely different situation. We do not recommend a MOM because you still have the opportunity to find the person by following the SOAR formula.

Leaving a MOM is the last resort. The reason being, if you *cop out* and start just leaving a series of MOMs, you will be back to waiting for return calls. It's important to remember that when you leave a MOM you remember who you called and are prepared with your strategy for the return MOM call.

Leaving a MOM is not as difficult as *receiving* a MOM. Receiving a MOM requires a humble approach and sophisticated talk trac. In the event you choose to leave a MOM, you must do so as stated so you create a positive "connection" with the person who will be calling you back. (Corporations have been using this MOM technique successfully for years without issue . . . provided it is executed correctly.)

Leaving a MOM vs. Receiving a MOM

Leaving a MOM

1. "Hello, [the person's name you are calling]. This is [your name]. I have been trying to reach you and haven't had much luck."

2. (The request) "If you could call me back I would appreciate it. It's 9 a.m. right now [whatever time it is], and I will be available until 3:30 [or whatever time applies]." (This implies urgency. Make the time you will be available about four hours or so.)

3. (Leave your number) "My number is [List the number. But, don't finish leaving the entire number . . . interrupt yourself and say, "better yet, let me give you my *direct cell number*. That number is . . ." Do not leave your company number. "Direct cell" implies importance; it's like saying, "let me give you the number to the yacht. There generally is no "direct cell" . . . it's the same as a cell. It just sounds more important. Also, be certain that the outgoing voice message on your personal cell is professional and does not mention your company. Additionally, make sure that the message on your cell for all incoming callers is professional.]

4. (Second request) "Again, I would appreciate it if you would return my call."

5. "Once again this is [your name]. I look forward to your call."

Tips for Leaving a Successful MOM

- When you leave your callback number, begin by starting to leave your corporate number, then *hesitate* and suggest your direct cell. This must be done with authenticity. You can't just rattle off the first number and then say the second number fast; it requires timing and melodic word delivery.

- Use voice intonation, hesitations, and so forth.

- Speak slowly.

- Use the prospect's name.

- When you leave a MOM, you should make a notation on the back of your cell phone so when the call comes in you know who is returning your call. An easy way is to simply put a piece of tape on the back of your cell phone with the name of the person you have left the MOM with. The incoming call may come when you least expect it. (When you receive the MOM callback, if you don't know who the call is coming from because you failed to make a note on your cell phone, you will stammer and odds are the caller will hang up. A quick peek at the tape will tell the tale!)

- You shouldn't have more than a few MOMs on the back of your cell phone at any given time, since you are supposed to be making *contact*, not just taking the easy way out and leaving MOMs.

- Practice leaving a MOM just like actors practice their lines. Be sure you deliver your MOM authentically. You don't want to sound as though you are reading from a script.

Note: Leaving a successful MOM means leaving very little key information, whereas an unsuccessful MOM provides information that reveals everything during the message.

Receiving a MOM

1. "Thanks for returning my call, [person's name]."

2. "I know my message may have been a little confusing, but because of all the *change* going on in today's market, I wanted to reach out to you . . ."

3. "I am with [your company]. We are a [describe your company/what they do]."

4. ". . . and the reason I was calling was [state your value statement]."

Tips for Receiving a Successful MOM

- Be grateful for the return call and be humble.

- Speak slowing and thank the person for calling you back.

- Acknowledge that your message may have been a little confusing (because it was).

- State that you are calling because of all the *change* in the market, then introduce your company and your value statement or the reason you are calling.

Note: if the client becomes annoyed with you, then you can be assured that the way you handled the incoming call was ineffective or not as instructed. You may have gone too fast, immediately started selling, or perhaps you didn't sound sincere. SOAR clients have left hundreds of MOMs with amazing success because they did so from an ethical approach and delivered the MOM as recommended.

Summary

Key points about leaving a MOM (message of mystery) when you are out of contact options:

- Leave a MOM on a client's business line or the client's business cell phone if you have it.
- Your callback number should be your cell number, not your business line.
- The message you have recorded on your personal cell must be professional in the event you miss the incoming MOM.
- When leaving a MOM, consider sticking a piece of tape with the name of the person you left the MOM with on the back of your cell phone.
- Incoming MOMs are to be treated with humility and exactly as scripted.
- MOMs are approximately 80 to 85 percent effective and are usually returned within 24 hours.
- If your incoming MOM caller is upset, it will likely have to do with your voice and the fact you did not follow script. Very few incoming calls from a MOM are upset.
- Practice your outgoing and incoming MOMs with a fellow salesperson before you leave one live.
- Leaving more than a few MOMs now and then may indicate you are taking the easy way out and not riding the bull.

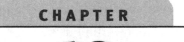

SOCIAL NETWORKING
USING SOAR

How LinkedIn "Links" With SOAR

The ability to effectively combine your LinkedIn tools with SOAR strategies can create a powerful business development tool. LinkedIn provides an exceptional platform that works in parallel with any research you may do before dialing. When you complete research on an organization's website, you are able to come away with "general" information that supports an initial net new dial. However, LinkedIn can give you more and provide you with a magnified personal view of a particular individual you would like to reach.

The Power of LinkedIn

LinkedIn allows you to obtain an understanding of the decision maker's personal and professional background, discover mutual connections, find the link to the company website, and anything else you may find useful about the person with whom you want to connect. Utilizing your mutual connections can be significant in establishing credibility for yourself while also driving net new business.

How the SOAR Formula
Works With Social Media

New connections on LinkedIn will create a "warm" call list, and these new connections can provide you with another reason to pick up the phone. Implementing the SOAR method allows you to bridge your LinkedIn connection with a conversation over the phone with the decision maker. If you implement the SOAR tactics correctly (diffusing the receptionist's *chip* so you can get to the decision maker, developing and conveying your value statement appropriately, handling objections, etc.), your result should be an appointment.

By accessing LinkedIn, you complete a necessary first step with your research before picking up the phone, since LinkedIn allows you to find common areas of interest (such as college education, similar career history, affiliated with the Alumni, similar professional interests, etc.) that you can use to develop a compelling value statement and make a positive connection on your first contact. Additionally, LinkedIn provides you with a platform that allows you to continue to build the relationship once the initial contact has been made.

Hint: Oftentimes you will come across the organization's corporate initiative. This will allow you to script a compelling value statement that is unique to the target you are calling.

A Potential Pitfall When Combining LinkedIn With SOAR

If your LinkedIn network has contacts that are not authentic and you don't have a *real* relationship with the shared connection between you and the decision maker, the effectiveness of this tool greatly decreases. As a result, your call can instantly go from a warm call to a cold call.

I remember that when we began with LinkedIn, we accepted nearly anyone who wanted to connect with us. We were told that it was best to "accept everyone, because the more contacts the better." As we learned, we began to eliminate those contacts that we were not familiar with and began to accept only those requests that we could validate. So, when using LinkedIn and SOAR, be sure the contacts you are reaching out to are reliable. Who you accept will ultimately be up to you, of course.

Summary

SOAR is a perfect match for a social networking approach. For example, when using LinkedIn, a salesperson may still have to make an initial telephone call. Receptionists may still be your greatest challenge for making contact despite the fact you are calling with a warm lead or social networking lead. The same thing applies when receiving a networking lead, which may provide a salesperson with a "warm lead"; you may still have to use the telephone.

Key points about using social networking with SOAR:

- The more you practice using the SOAR method with social networking, the more success is guaranteed.
- LinkedIn is an excellent source of research prior to using SOAR.
- By using social networking, you will be able to craft a more unique value statement.
- LinkedIn allows you to better understand the prospect's objectives and arrive at a more magnified view of the person you are calling.
- Bottom line: you can "get in" up to 90 percent of the time on any net dial.

The one thing we know about sales managers is that they want their sales team to drive revenue and that one of the areas that can generate net new business is *effective prospecting* (this includes prospecting through social networking). Yet, most salespeople attempt prospecting only to become frustrated with poor results and, subsequently, they often avoid finding net new business altogether. SOAR will help you and provide a powerful solution to *driving net new business*. SOAR Selling does this in two ways: first, by adjusting the mindset of your sales team, and second, by providing powerful techniques for making contact with decision makers and high influencers. What we have found with SOAR is that matching a powerful mindset with a winning formula equals a successful contact methodology. SOAR Selling provides both the mindset and the techniques.

When it comes to prospecting, most salespeople struggle. However, once they are face-to-face with customers, they often demonstrate that they are well versed in what to do. There are numerous big name selling programs around that tell salespeople what they should do "once they get in," but there is little instruction on "*how* to get in." Currently, the prevailing prospecting strategy is one that is familiar to us all: *just make lots of calls and you will eventually make contact.* We call it BTN + L (By The Numbers + Luck.) It's a brutal strategy that drives attrition (and, often, unethical tactics), but up until now there have been very few alternatives. Yes, there are other forms of driving net new business, but when you want to make contact with someone *now* and do so efficiently, the SOAR formula provides a proven and ethical solution.

There are countless journals and articles by top training organizations telling salespeople how to prospect. Many of these articles have a catchy title, like, *Getting Past Gatekeepers:*

Everything You Need to Know or *How to Get Your Foot in the Door* and so on. In reality, few of these articles actually tell the salesperson *how to make contact.*

With SOAR, the salespeople on your team actually have a step-by-step approach when it comes to making contact and getting appointments with decision makers. In this book, we tell you "how to get through." No lies, no smoke and mirrors . . . just straight talk! The SOAR formula works; it has been demonstrated consistently in multiple industries and cultures over the past two decades. As you get deeper into the SOAR methodologies, you will find amazing answers. As part of the SOAR selling strategy, it's important to review the six biggest mistakes that sales professionals make when it comes to prospecting.

The Top Six Telephone Prospecting Voids

1. Not Knowing *How* to Make Contact on Initial Dials

As we suggested, it is astonishing to discover that many organizations offer little instruction to their sales force on *how to reach decision makers* on the telephone. As a result, salespeople make the effort, dialing only to eventually hang up because the receptionist says things like, "I don't believe he is in," or "she didn't answer," or "what is this regarding?" or "is he expecting your call?" Since salespeople are not trained in how to handle these scenarios, they often misinterpret the response by the receptionist and hang up. This pattern continues throughout the day with the salesperson making dozens, even hundreds, of calls, seeking to eventually "get lucky" by making contact using the BTN + L approach.

The end result of this discouraging process is low performance and often high attrition. Many sales managers blame their salespeople for lackluster results since they believe prospecting is "just a numbers game" and the salesperson who is struggling just isn't cutting it. And unfortunately, the end result is that quality salespeople are released from organizations for poor performance, when in fact it's often a matter of training.

2. Not Having a Compelling Value Statement

When salespeople do make contact on a net new call, they often don't know what to say! In our research, we learned that, despite being with a well-respected firm, many salespeople were often ill-equipped when it came to delivering a compelling *value statement*. We know that most organizations' focus is on driving net new business, yet they often offer limited training on the mechanics of prospecting or the importance of delivering a compelling value statement. Many organizations who hire salespeople believe that, because a salesperson comes with experience, he or she certainly knows how to prospect . . . big mistake.

In live trainings, we often ask sales attendees to break into teams and draft two or three value statements they could use on a live dial. The next day, the attendees choose the value statements they believe to be the best. The results are frequently similar. Time after time, they chose value statements that were overly complicated and often written in a long paragraph format. In truth, the best value statement is often short and to the point. When value statements are lengthy, the target prospect hears *reading*, which takes away natural delivery and the sincerity of the value statement. It's the key nuggets of the value statement that make the most impact.

3. Not Being Prepared to Handle Objections

Through our research, we found that, once the target contact began to ask questions or state objections, only the best of the best salespeople prevailed. Essentially, the senior salespeople would handle objections with ease, while the rookies and mid-players got crushed. Many new to mid-level salespeople are sent to the battlefield with very little training in objection handling. It made us wonder how many opportunities were lost simply because a salesperson couldn't get past objections. We discovered that, instead of *hearing the objection* and evolving the conversation, salespeople simply did what they thought they were supposed to do and trained to do, and that is: sell, sell, sell!

As further evidence of this, when we receive random calls from solicitors to *our* company, we will provide them with an objection to see how they handle it . . . only to have them hang up. It's crazy and, from our point of view, it damages the world of selling. Salespeople often struggle with objections; when the call gets more complex, the only thing they know to do is start selling over the objections or cut the call short by offering to send something—or as we said, sometimes they just hang up!

4. Not Qualifying During the First Call

It was interesting to discover during live training calls that if a new prospect said, "send me something" (SMS), the salesperson would simply comply without any level of qualifying to determine if the SMS was authentic. Even if a client would agree to an appointment, the salespeople simply set the appointment without much investigation. Lack of *qualifying* produces an unreliable pipeline. Many salespeople actually believed they had a *live prospect* simply because the contact said, "send me something." When we train during SOAR, we ask salespeople what they *think* when a target client makes that statement. Invariably, salespeople respond with, "it means they aren't interested," or "it means they are trying to get rid of you," and so forth. We then ask them, "how do you know that's what *send me something* means?" They begin to really think. We discovered there is a notion out there among salespeople that "send me something" means there is no interest, because all the target client is trying to do is get rid of you. As a result, many potential transactions are lost. It's not that the salespeople aren't smart or patient . . . it's simply a matter of inadequate training with regards to *listening, interpretation, and qualifying* what is being said to them.

5. Not Differentiating

We used to work in the commercial real estate world, so we know the industry quite well. As a result, we are always amused when we receive telephone solicitation from a commercial broker. Since brokers don't know that we were in the business, we listen carefully to their value statement only to learn that they all tend to say the same thing. Not a stitch of differentiation! We liken it to the behavior of a cow: just follow the herd . . . no getting off the trail . . . do what everyone else does. Those that follow the herd will attain success in some cases; it's just that they do so by not giving up rather than through differentiating. We have to admire their determination to stay the course in the face of adversity, but just think what would have happened to them if they had learned to *differentiate* early on. The most successful salespeople we know attribute a significant amount of their success to having *differentiated* themselves; that is, they've found a new way to solve a problem or set themselves apart from the competition.

6. Not Getting an Appointment on the First Call

Once again, most organizations believe that if a salesperson has been selling for more than a few years, he certainly knows how to reach decision makers and get appointments. We have discovered that this is typically not the case. Repeatedly, we witness salespeople of all levels missing opportunities to secure an appointment on a first call/contact. It's amazing to hear dialogue between a salesperson and a new prospect target. Oftentimes the target prospects send out the signal that they are open for an appointment, and the salesperson just doesn't hear it! (During live calling, the SOAR instructor coaching the salesperson on the telephone is frantically signaling, "get the appointment!") As we said, it happens to both rookies and experienced salespeople. After salespeople hang up, we ask the class, "was there an appointment there?" The answer is frequently yes! Maybe it's fear of rejection, or maybe the pressure of dialing in front of others *live* dead-ends the appointment. For the most part, we believe the problem is a matter of intention and training. Prior to the live call, we always ask the salespeople what their objective is, and invariably we hear things like, "I want to get information," or "I want to see if they need anything." Interestingly, they don't often say, "I want to get an appointment!"

With constant encouragement from our instructors to get an appointment, we are beginning to see a shift from a low percentage of appointments to an appointment rate often above 40 percent on every net new dial. After training a SOAR class, one of our clients was getting a discouraging 8 percent appointments on each new contact made. We subsequently delivered a concentrated, intense value statement and objection-handling training specifically for their company. Following the value statement training, they were achieving a 37 percent appointment average on every live dial. That's a 362 percent increase! Since the Dialexis instructors now focus more intently on getting appointments, not just making contact, we are delighted to see appointments on first dials creeping above the 30 percent mark to as much as 50 percent or more on first contact. Just think what that can do to organizations' revenue.

As we travel the world teaching SOAR, the same voids appear repeatedly in diverse industries, with all levels of salespeople, corporate cultures, and in different countries. More than just pitfalls, these are huge crevasses where most sales opportunities are irretrievably lost during prospecting.

Why Senior Salespeople Stop Prospecting

1. A Perception That It's for Rookies

When salespeople start out as rookies, they usually enter the company with a compliant attitude. They realize they don't have the experience others may have in the organization and, as a result, they are wide open to taking direction. They want to be successful and are excited about the prospect of doing well. At the start of a selling career, rookies often exhibit the best attitude they will ever have in their career. They know they have to pay the price, as others have before them, so they are up to any task. It's amazing how humble they are. They are told that one of the keys to winning requires developing accounts through driving net new business. If they don't have enough pipeline or closings, they are told to simply make more calls;

once again, it's BTN + L at work. They are told to fill the funnel with more and more calls, and eventually they will win. We have seen organizations that require their salespeople to make as many as 100 calls a day! Just dial, dial, dial! It's a brutal approach, but rookies do it for one simple reason: they were told to and, since they acknowledge the fact that they are rookies, they endure the pain. If it ends up that they can no longer take the abuse a BTN + L approach yields, the sales manager may suggest they aren't cut out for sales. However, if salespeople can stick in there and handle all the difficulties a BTN + L formula serves up, they really do eventually make money and can succeed. After a few years of this crushing approach, they may finally have clients that are consistently producing. Essentially, they now have what we call *oil wells*. At last, they are free from having to BTN + L and the amazing pressure they have endured, and—you guessed it—they drop prospecting for net new business as fast as they can. After all, they suffered cold calling the only way they knew, through BTN + L, and now they have "arrived"; they are becoming experienced salespeople. Since they now have oil wells, they justify they no longer need to prospect. Besides, they are clear that looking for net new business by calling cold is for rookies.

Common reasons why oil wells dry up are:

- The company changes its strategy.

- The salesperson's key contact retires, dies, quits, gets fired, or is wooed away.

- The competition slides in with a better offer.

- The salesperson quits and the account shifts to another organization.

- The company goes out of business.

2. Claimed Lack of Time

We realize that, once a salesperson is considered senior, she can get pretty busy. After all, those oil wells are producing results and generating lots of paperwork, so when would she have the time to drive net new business by calling new prospects? Besides, senior salespeople often justify not driving lead generation through prospecting because they believe it's for rookies. Senior salespeople already did it when they were rookies, and now that they are successful, why would they want to go back to something like BTN + L?

Of course, we all know what happens: *all oil wells dry up*. When the oil wells dry up, senior salespeople can be caught off guard, and as we have seen over the years, it is a humbling experience. When oil wells dry up everyone takes a hit. The company loses consistent revenue, the salesperson loses revenue and stature, and ultimately someone may lose a job. The tragedy is, the senior salesperson really didn't have to go back to BTN + L; all they really had to do was make a few *net new* calls each week using a technique like SOAR, and they would have found new wells! That would have taken little time. Think about it: only three net new dials per day (or even per week) would most likely be sufficient to find new wells if the calling is done correctly. *The time it takes to make three net new SOAR dials is approximately one hour.* SOAR will connect you with a decision maker or high influencer, resulting in a conversation; in those cases the calls take longer because you are making contact. Any senior salesperson can give one hour a day or a week to find new wells!

A True Story

We were teaching a prospecting class when, in the middle of the session, the number one salesperson raised his hand and stated flatly, "I'm not trying to be rude, but I think prospecting is for *new* salespeople. Some of us have little need to cold call anymore."

This particular salesperson was very experienced: the top company producer, he made $250,000 a year (this was 20 years ago) with 90 percent of his revenue coming from one account. You can guess the rest of the story. His one big oil well dried up six months after the SOAR training, and he personally hit bottom. It happened, as it always does, without warning—no e-mail, phone call, or even a smoke signal. About this time, when we returned to the company to complete more training, this same salesperson volunteered to take us to the airport after the session. Subsequently he apologized for being so arrogant the first time around and admitted to being in a world of hurt. He said he had forgotten how to prospect and was scared that he couldn't cut it in sales anymore. He no longer believed in perpetual oil wells. (Although his humility was restored, he ultimately washed out of the industry.) Save your organization and your salespeople from this kind of devastating loss! Keep your teams prospecting consistently. Make it mandatory and measure it; make it part of your sales culture. Install the SOAR accountability process so you can measure ROI. As the saying goes, "You can never be too rich, or too thin." Maybe we should add, or have too many "oil wells."

3. Lack of Accountability

Most of us do not do that which we detest, and most salespeople detest driving net new business! Because of this mindset, the last thing a senior salesperson will want to do is make a prospecting call, and without accountability, it usually doesn't happen. Sales management often has the view that they don't need to hold *senior* salespeople accountable for demand generation because of one key reason: they are senior. Experienced salespeople are given wide berth, and understandably so; after all they generally produce, they don't need to be micromanaged and sales managers are often slammed with so many other responsibilities they don't have the time to hold salespeople accountable. The last thing they want to do is hold senior salespeople accountable for driving net new business if they are already hitting their numbers. Where's the logic in that? We know the answer, because we said it earlier: all oil wells dry up. If there is no accountability for driving new business, it probably won't happen.

Consider this: do you think it's possible that sales managers don't hold salespeople accountable for demand generation because they themselves once did it and remember how much they hated it? As a result, they may go easy on the salesperson because they understand how hard it was and have become compassionate. If you think that's possible, don't you wonder what other aspects of a salesperson's development may be held back by unconscious sales management "beliefs"?

4. A Belief That Telephone Prospecting Doesn't Work—Especially "Calling Cold"

There may be better ways for you to drive net new business; we wouldn't know your personal situation. We're not saying using the telephone is the only way, it's just *a way*. We realize that demand generation can be achieved through the following, as well:

1. Networking

2. Peer Group

3. Existing Account Expansion

4. Social Media

5. E-mail campaigns

6. Advertising

7. Mailings

8. Creative Approaches

9. Trade Shows, Conferences

10. Company Leads (if there are any!)

A True Story

We were working with a large client that offered *retired* executives the opportunity to begin a consulting group. After two weeks of intense SOAR training at the corporate offices, the executives were to return to their home base and contact other *active* executives to join their new consulting group. This required the retired executives to immediately contact candidates as quickly as possible upon return home. The sooner they were successful, the sooner they would be able to support others and generate income. One of the ways the retired executives were encouraged to connect with potential CEO candidates was through peer relationships, networking, mailings, social media, e-mail, and cold prospecting. Of course, calling cold was the least favorite method. As a matter of fact, it was more than the "least favorite;" it was resisted. As a result, this approach was the very last strategy relied upon to find new members. Once home, the executives burned through every possible connection they had, sent hundreds of mailings, fired off loads of e-mails and when all attempts to find new candidates were completed, they then had no other choice but to turn to using SOAR! It's all they had left because they didn't enroll enough new members. In the end, it was proven that the SOAR formula generated 80 percent of their new members. The oldest method in the book, calling cold, was the most successful. All is well that ends well . . . but just think how many months were lost by avoiding using SOAR as a method for making contact!

Below in Figure BM-1, there are some well-articulated excuses that salespeople give to their manager.

Salesperson says:	Manager hears:	The possible reality:
I don't have time.	The salesperson is really busy and will get to it when they can.	Salesperson is disorganized.
Prospecting is for rookies.	The salesperson is senior, so they have a good point; plus, they prospect within their key accounts.	Salesperson's a prima donna, because of it, they are at risk of losing the company's key accounts.
I'm going to do it.	Salesperson is going to do it.	It's not happening.
Calling cold doesn't work.	The salesperson is right.	Salesperson doesn't know how to use calling cold effectively.
I'm the top salesperson and I bring in big bucks, so I don't have time to prospect.	If I push too hard, I may lose the salesperson, they may go to the competition.	All oil wells dry up. The salesperson and the company are at risk for account loss.
I'm doing it.	Salesperson is doing it.	Salesperson probably isn't doing it.
I can't handle more business.	Salesperson is carrying a heavy load—they don't have time to prospect.	Work can be handed off. Making at least one net new contact a week is something even big time salespeople can do.
I will prospect.	Salesperson will be getting on it.	Without measurement you will never know.
I'm buried in paperwork.	There is a lot of paperwork, so it's probably true.	The salesperson is unorganized. If they bury themselves in paperwork, they won't have to bury themselves in driving net new business!
Jeff and I are doing a blitz day this week.	These guys mean business.	Occasional blitz days typically don't make it, it has to be a consistent effort to be successful and sustainable—not a now and again blitz day!

Figure BM-1 *Well-Articulated Excuses*

Solutions for Increasing a Salesperson's Interest in Driving Net New Business

1. **Provide the best skill development available.** Prospecting is perceived to be hard, and to a great extent the way salespeople prospect *makes* it hard. SOAR makes it easy, and it's a proven formula that if followed will produce results. That doesn't mean salespeople will like it; it's just that it's *easier*. The concept that salespeople don't prospect because they're lazy or stubborn isn't necessarily accurate from our point of view. It's usually avoidance associated with ineffective skills or negative beliefs about prospecting. So if you expect salespeople to drive net new business, it is critical to provide them with skills that really work. SOAR is the one powerful application that changes the prospecting game dramatically.

2. **Be fair about the number of contacts and appointments you expect.** Remember the story about the salesperson that told his manager that he made 100 calls a day? The manager replied, "Fantastic!" The salesperson replied, "I could have made 150 calls, but two people asked me a question!" Think in terms of *quality*, not quantity! With the SOAR formula, your sales team will make fewer calls and be much more successful. When prospecting the old or traditional way, through BTN + L, a salesperson has to make numerous calls before making contact. And the numbers we hear relative to making contact is outrageously low—maybe 10 to 20 percent of the time. As of this writing, SOAR has a documented contact rate with a decision maker or someone of high influence 90 percent of every net dial!

3. **Train your salespeople on what to say *once they make contact*.** It sounds rather fundamental, but we find salespeople: (a) Are astounded when they make contact or (b) Say foolish things when making contact. Typically, rookies don't have a prayer. It seems so simple: make contact . . . say something compelling . . . get an appointment . . . close a transaction. Believe it or not, the

tough part is learning how to make contact and knowing what to say once the prospect answers. Your salespeople need help in developing a compelling value statement. If you think your salespeople are different, make a few calls with them; listen to each call and see the results they get. Of course, there are talented salespeople that have the ability to deliver a sound value statement when reaching a prospect, but it's not the norm. After two decades of making calls with top-notch firms in North America and Europe, we've seen that most salespeople have very little experience in value statement creation or delivery.

4. **Show your salespeople how to handle objections.** Salespeople appreciate knowing the answers to the most challenging objections prospects give. Sales managers are generally under the assumption that their sales force knows the answers. When it comes to the senior salespeople, they are probably right. It's the mid-level and rookie group that need help. It's an easy problem to solve.

5. **Watch your salespeople dial.** We find the best way to support a salesperson's dialing effectiveness is to *watch them dial*. It reveals a great deal and provides you with specific developmental recommendations. If approved by your firm, consider making mutual calls on a speakerphone or a dual telephone system so you can hear both sides of the conversation. As a side note, in a live SOAR class, Dialexis trainers use speakerphones for the dialing portion of the course. In all the years of dialing using a speakerphone, we have had less than minimal issues. I know you may be thinking that a prospect will object to being on a speakerphone; however, it doesn't seem to present a problem (perhaps because the speakerphones manufactured today are of high quality). Whatever the case, we can count on one hand the times when a prospect asked not be on a speakerphone. Additionally, since the calls *are not being* recorded when our trainers conduct live dialing in class, organizations have no objection to the use of a speakerphone. Dialexis did have one Fortune 500 client who

did not want the live dialing segment of SOAR to be executed on speakerphone, so our instructors used a different technique for making the live calls in class; the success rate of SOAR was the same. However, if you are choosing to coach your salespeople it is valuable to hear both sides of the conversation. Check with your organization to determine if speakerphone use is accepted.

6. **Hold your sales team accountable.**   Once again, holding salespeople accountable for driving net new business is challenging for many sales managers. We have discovered that checking in now and then isn't effective. It takes *consistent* attention to determine if the job is getting done. What we found is that an easy way to be consistent is to use the SOAR measurement process through your CRM. The reasons are clear: salespeople don't like to drive net new business because it is more challenging than simply handling the existing accounts they have. As a result, it's essential to hold your people accountable.

One of the challenges sales managers face is dealing with the massive amounts of information and a myriad of things that distract them from tracking results. The bottom line is that the sales manager often assumes the job is getting done when in fact it isn't or, often, not to the degree that will make a difference at the end of each month or quarter or whatever the reporting cycle is.

7. **Find out what your salespeople want and help them get it.** When you discover a salesperson's personal motivator, the thing that is the most important to him, and you then show him that prospecting or finding net new business will help him get what he wants, you will see intention and focus for demand generation increase. Think of it this way: why does a circus lion jump through a ring of fire? It is not because the lion fears the ringmaster or his whip since he can easily overcome both. It's not to please the crowd; the lion doesn't care about the crowd. We all know why: the lion is motivated by food. More important, the *right* food. When you discover what your salespeople want

and show them how to get it, you will have discovered how to inspire them to increase their interest in driving net new business. Once that happens, they will constantly develop new oil wells and protect themselves and the organization from client attrition! We know the fear of job loss will cause action as well, but it's not the same emotional connection. What you want to do is to connect to your salespeople's passions and use prospecting for new business as a vehicle to help them get what they reveal their passion is. Fear and pain will often motivate a salesperson to prospect; however, in the long run that approach represents a losing formula. Motivation that is lasting will emanate from knowing their dreams—what they want for their families and what they want for themselves. So, find out what each of your salespeople are motivated by and "why" and then show them how driving net new business will help them achieve their business and *personal* goals.

8. **Increase accountability.**   Let's face it. Most salespeople have good intentions. When your sales force tells you they will deliver their sales quota, they believe they will. They want to be successful. They start the month off all fired up, but then get caught up in countless details, paperwork, rejections, and self-destructive techniques, resulting in missed quotas. You hear the well-articulated excuse for the umpteenth time. Some of these excuses are very creative, but most of them you've heard a thousand times before. You may have even used a couple of these excuses yourself when you were in sales. If salespeople realize they will be measured and held accountable, their prospecting changes dramatically. Measurement is a mandate when it comes to creating results. Your team doesn't need to be blamed or made to feel inadequate. They just need to know that you expect them to achieve certain measurable results on a daily or weekly basis, no exceptions. They need to know what's expected and that they will be held accountable for meeting those expectations.

The Achilles' Heel Factor

Unfortunately, we have found sales managers may not know how to prospect any better than the salespeople that they are leading because they may have been out of the field for years. As a result, when salespeople reach out for assistance, the sales manager might respond with BTN + L (By The numbers + Luck). Essentially what they are saying is, "just make a lot of calls and you'll be fine." Most likely that is how they were trained. That is an approach, but it doesn't support the salesperson much and it is a great contributor to missed forecasting and attrition. When sales managers learn how to SOAR, they discover how to coach using a compelling formula. Subsequently, the results astound both the sales manager and the salesperson!

Why Blitz Days May Not Solve the Problem

It's not that "blitz" days don't work, it's just that they are typically infrequent. They are thought of as a "fun day," making them not as efficient as if they were part of the culture of the organization. When salespeople don't prospect continually, the pressure builds up, the guilt builds up, and then it is all supposed to be resolved in a "blitz" day. Another issue is that the "blitz" day only seems to come up once in a millennium. If you are having "blitz" days every week, then you are at least doing something. One suggestion is to make driving *new logos* a consistent practice, not a now-and-then event. Consistency changes habits. Since we know well that salespeople don't like to prospect, it's going to take more than a "blitz day" to get significant pipeline results.

As we have said, most salespeople are encouraged on their "blitz" days to use the old formula of BTN + L, just make tons of calls, and eventually make contact. It's true: if salespeople make enough calls, the odds are they will make contact. But it actually demotivates the spirit for driving new business.

Salespeople join an organization, are trained on product knowledge, and then are told to go find new business. They are given an inaccurate prospecting list, which leads to discouragement. As a result, they move toward networking, social media, and a now and then attempt at making a few prospecting calls. The system is broken because of the inaccurate list and the salesperson's lack of knowledge on how to find new business. As a result, the new salesperson gets discouraged, tries to stay just under the radar, and is not as successful as she could be. Driving net new business ends up taking a backseat.

With SOAR, a salesperson can reach decision makers with amazing results. For example: under the old way of prospecting, if a salesperson wanted to make 10 new contacts in a day, he may have to make 50 dials or more, essentially yielding a 20 percent contact rate. With SOAR, a salesperson would only need to make 12 net dials to reach 10 decision makers or high influencers! It's an amazing shift, but it's true.

Why Salespeople May Not Have a Closing Problem

Every time we ask a group of sales managers what they think is most lacking in a salesperson's arsenal besides consistently bringing in net new business, new logos, or new business from an exisitng account, one of the most common replies is: *closing skills.*

It's always the same: sales managers in particular believe that closing skills represent the biggest issue when it comes to salespeople not closing business. From a Dialexis point of view, that's not always the case. Our view is that there is no mysterious closing technique that a salesperson can use that causes a prospect to suddenly sign the deal. From all our years of training throughout the world and personal experience, we have never heard of some "magical" thing to say that makes the prospect close the deal. The majority of the time the significant reason transactions don't close has to do with inadequate qualifying, not closing techniques.

We have seen it time and time again during prospecting calls on the telephone and on the street: salespeople just don't qualify. When we teach live dialing in SOAR, we hear the target contact say those farmiliar words, "send me something." Our instructors then have the opportunity to wittnes the salespersons response, which is almost always, "OK." Then: *click*. This happens all the time.

The next thing that transpires is the salespeople hustle out a SMS (send me something), then log that SMS into their pipeline and report it to their manager as a potential deal. The problem is the deal rarely closes! Why? Because it was never a deal! *Most SMS requests are not deals*! As a matter of fact, the SMS may equal NI: not interested! The salesperson's view of SMS is that a prospect is not interested; "it's just to get them off the phone." Yet, the salespeople put the SMS on their "prospect" list or in their pipeline of potential new business. It becomes more of a pipe*dream* than a pipeline.

The only way to know if an SMS is authentic is to qualify it. The end result is, lots of deals in the pipe and no substantial net new business or revenue to report. The sales manager ends up looking foolish because he has submitted the anticipated revenue and the salesperson is crushed because she isn't making the money she wants. Not qualifying leads to a loss all the way around.

When you experience SOAR, you will most likely be blown away. SOAR is a new tool that will support you in finding net new business or reach almost anyone you wish with a level of success you've never experienced before. You will more than likely become like many before you: amazed and transformed. SOAR will deliver a hard and soft ROI (return on investment of time and money) to you and your organization. The soft ROI will be the mindset segment of the material, essentially offering you a transformational bridge to higher performance. It's powerful, lasting, and it complements the formula for executing SOAR. It will provide you with a solid platform for a substantial break-through in your thinking. You will be astounded at how you can turn your mindset into a powerful force for top 20 percent+ achievement in your selling career and beyond. This will represent a significant piece of your overall strategy in taking your career to the top, making the money, and finding the independence or recognition you are looking for. If nothing else, this new methodology along with the mindset segment will give you an extra layer of protection from client attrition.

Secondly, the SOAR formula will provide you with a real-world system that is extremely unique for making contact with decision makers and gaining more appointments, which will lead to net new business! The contact rate SOAR delivers is up to 90 percent on every *net* dial, meaning that every time you make a *net* dial you have the possibility of making contact with a decision maker or high influencer up to 90 percent of the time! It dramatically shifts finding new business verses the old way of prospecting. The 90 percent plus number is constantly updated by live trainings, so that percentage moves. The SOAR *minimum* contact rate is considered to be 70 percent, but that is rare. In live SOAR classes we have often seen a 100 percent contact rate. It's not only the technology of SOAR "talk trac," but also SOAR mindset—that's often the distinction between a 90 percent contact rate and a 100 percent contact rate! When everyone in the class makes a personal commitment to make 100 percent contact on the live *cold* dials in class, you'd be surprised how powerful that commitment is in delivering an amazing contact and appointment percentage.

Myths and Truths of Driving Net New Business

MYTH: Cold call telephone prospecting doesn't work

TRUTH: If you find yourself thinking that cold telephone prospecting doesn't work, you are probably right. But this is only because you have most likely experienced the "old way" of prospecting. If you are implementing the BTN + L (by the numbers + luck) way of prospecting, then it would make sense why it's not working for you. If you are using SOAR, however, the game changes significantly. It not only works to drive net new business, it produces immediate opportunity!

MYTH: Cold calling is best for small account penetration.

TRUTH: It's powerful for enterprise account penetration, also, when combined with pre-research.

MYTH: Cold calling is hard.

TRUTH: Most would say this is accurate, but when driving net new business using the SOAR techniques, you will experience a world of difference. Stay with the old way of prospecting and it can be brutal.

MYTH: Prospecting *within* the account is better than driving new logos.

TRUTH: Prospecting *within* the account is a great way to grow business, but if the account dries up you may find yourself in a panic, scrambling for your next new account. The only protection you have is to continue to look for new logos!

MYTH: Cold calling is considered an ancient approach to driving business.

TRUTH: Many training companies or outside training gurus say things like, "cold calling is for dummies," or "cold calling is dead." It makes sense when we hear that because as we said, "most corporations are prospecting by telephone using the old method of cold calling, BTN + L (by the numbers + luck)." This method is not only rarely effective, but also devastating to the salesperson.

MYTH: No one likes unsolicited calls.

TRUTH: Some executives may not, but millions *accept* this process. It's about your value statement, your value statement delivery, and how you conduct yourself on the call.

MYTH: In order to be successful at pure *cold* telephone prospecting, you have to bend the rules to some degree or it's too hard.

TRUTH: The BTN + L approach creates unethical strategies. SOAR represents an ethical and highly professional approach for driving net new business—and it works! Dishonesty never works as a strategy, and if you use dishonesty to be successful, it will not only ruin your organization's reputation, but yours as well.

MYTH: It's tough to get past the gatekeeper.

TRUTH: Not with SOAR! In fact, it's actually easy.

MYTH: There is nothing anyone can do when it comes to voice mail.

TRUTH: Surprise! There is a lot you can do. Voice mail is not considered a block when using SOAR.

Why Salespeople Hate to Prospect

It's easy to dislike prospecting cold or even warm; most salespeople do, primarily because it's the way you have been trained (or haven't been trained) that makes it hard. As a result, salespeople make dozens of calls before they talk to a warm body, and that's not fun. Who wants to sit and dial day in, day out with limited success? Worse than that, once you make contact, you may not have the right message or value statement to stimulate interest. That's a common problem for many salespeople. You make dial after dial after dial after dial to reach one decision maker . . . but once you get lucky you often strike out with your value statement. It's a pretty discouraging reality. On top of all that, your colleagues will be right there to tell you it's a waste of time! Salespeople need a proven system to be successful, one that works.

Though you may never love prospecting, the SOAR approach can make it tolerable by producing results faster. Reaching a decision maker or high influencer up to 90 percent of every net dial and combined with the proper value statement will increase appointments. If these appointments are qualified, the results will produce a net new business increase, and that's what it's all about. All you need to do to shift your prospecting results with SOAR are two things: change your mindset and shift your tactics to the new way of driving revenue. Then, watch your net new business accelerate!

15 Reasons Why Driving Net New Business Is Worth the Effort

1. You will do what you agreed to do when you took a selling position.

2. You will make more money.

3. You will protect your income from falling (remember: all oil wells go dry).

4. You will put yourself in a position to solve problems for new clients.

5. You will most likely move to the top 20 percent+ in your organization.

6. You will keep your pipeline full.

7. You will enjoy more business and personal security.

8. You will earn the respect of your colleagues and your organization.

9. You will gain positive market recognition.

10. You will increase market knowledge and market share.

11. You will keep your skills sharp.

12. You will differentiate yourself.

13. You will increase your influence.

14. You will feel an amazing level of growth and heightened self-esteem.

15. You will put yourself in a position to present your product or service professionally.

The Importance of Ethical Prospecting

One thing we are sure you will agree with is that prospecting has a tainted history. We're not surprised: when we think about how difficult prospecting is for salespeople, it's no wonder that some resort to unethical methods to make contact. If a salesperson is required to make hundreds of calls and those calls yield minimal results, the salesperson may eventually resort to overly aggressive tactics, and sometimes even unethical ones. The SOAR formula promotes an ethical approach to driving net new business. Applying SOAR as it is instructed results in a surprisingly high contact percentage while using an ethical approach. As a result, the pressure to make contact shifts dramatically.

Let's say your company requires 10 net new contacts per day. That means speaking with someone that is a decision maker or high influencer. With the old prospecting techniques, you may have to make as many as 50 to 100 calls . . . or even more! That's pretty discouraging. If you executed SOAR, you would only have to make 12 net dials to make those 10 contacts! That's right, 12 net dials, vs. 50 or 100 net dials . . . and that's doing it ethically! The truth is, you don't have to lie to make contact, you just need the right techniques. Being ethical matters since it's your reputation and your company's reputation that's on the line every day. You don't need to cheat, lie, or make up untruths.

Trust is the foundation for a successful sales career. Your reputation, your word, and a handshake are often thought of as the majority of your worth. Make sure your name and your organization's name are highly regarded. Always leave the account better than you found it. As a sales professional, it's your obligation to forward the career of selling as an admired profession. You do that by maintaining integrity.

A True Story

My partner and I were recently staying at a hotel and were sitting in the lobby. While there, we began a conversation with a professional looking woman who said she lived in New York. During the conversation, we exchanged what we did for a living and we learned that she was in sales. She told us that she represented a large (and well-known) University as a fund-raiser. When we told her, "We own a sales training company that is focused on teaching salespeople how to reach decision makers on the telephone," she lit up! She said, "Boy I could certainly use that information." She then said, "I hate to tell you this, but I lie! It's the only way I can get through the gatekeeper. I tell prospects that I know people I don't really know and often exaggerate the facts. It's the only way I know how to get it done."

We were shocked. She looked very professional, and we would have never guessed by her appearance that she would misrepresent herself or her University. We subsequently suggested we could help her, and she said she had to speak to someone across the room and would return with her card in a moment. She didn't. Additionally, when we were leaving the hotel to head for dinner out, we saw her sitting on a bench in front of the hotel talking to someone. As we passed by, we said hello and she said hello . . . no card.

Really disappointing and harmful to the world of selling. We wondered what the powers to be at her University would think if they knew how she was conducting herself.

Prospecting Isn't Just for Rookies

If you are an experienced salesperson, you realize that finding new business never ends—never. Whether you call it prospecting, networking, or expanding the white space, it doesn't matter—it's all the same, it's all about increasing your client base. That also means that, even if you are in enterprise sales contacting Fortune 100 or Fortune 50 accounts, or you have a specific market you are focused on, continuous prospecting matters. Oil wells dry up. You have seen it: companies merge, fall off the radar and move their business out of your territory . . . the reasons are limitless. If you are senior salesperson, you've been around the block, and you must recognize that your best account is currently being solicited by your competition—right now! And that's more fact than fiction. Every account you have is a target, and despite the power of the relationship you have with your top accounts and the quality of your offering, you are at risk every day, every hour, and every minute.

It takes a good deal of time to secure key accounts and seconds to lose them. Losing an account may have nothing to do with your personal performance or your organization's performance. You could be performing above standard and still lose the account or have an account shift their strategy or decide it's time to try another vendor. Sometimes it may be because your company isn't the leader in its field any longer. Again, there are a myriad of factors that cause an account to drop your line or shift to the competition.

Consider this: you most likely have health insurance, homeowner's insurance, or car insurance—but what about major account insurance? The only insurance available for major account protection is *prospecting for net new business*, and whether it's a warm lead or a personal introduction, you ultimately have to make the call. What we have seen that is drastically overlooked and can provide amazing return on effort (if done properly) is prospecting. Without new business generation, *you are at risk.*

Our view is that prospecting isn't just for rookies. In fact, when senior salespeople utilize the SOAR technology, they become lethal.

SOAR is for every salesperson who wants to be successful and stay successful. It's a great way to get to the top 20 percent+ and remain there, consistently.

How to Make Net New Prospecting Tolerable

With SOAR, you have a system that works, and as we said, "yields contact success up to 90 percent of every net dial." You may hate prospecting because you've been doing it the old way. It's why so many potentially great salespeople don't want to enter the field of selling.

Being successful when you dial makes prospecting tolerable. With the SOAR formula and mindset components, you will make fewer calls, enjoy more contacts, and ultimately be successful at driving net new business. It's been our experience that most salespeople will do almost anything, even if it's not fun, exciting, or even if it's barely tolerable, as long as the difficulty *leads them to their goals*. So, if you have a desire to be at the top of the charts as a salesperson, or build a nest egg for your family, or make enough money to support others—then the effort it takes to drive net new business can be a key element to your success and getting you to your goals. With your personal vision intact, you will then be motivated to do whatever it takes—and SOAR will be a valuable tool to support you.

When It's Critical to Research an Account Prior to Dialing

One of the most frequently asked questions during SOAR training continues to be, "is it best to just start calling prospects or research the account before dialing?" The answer is . . . it depends.

If your company is patient about sales results and the philosophy of your firm is more geared toward relationship building, then you may be able to take longer before getting started, which will allow you to do forward research. The key below should help shed some light on this question.

When You May Need to Start Calling Fast with Minimal Advance Research

- If you are expected to bring in net new business quickly because the culture of the organization is "results now!"

- If you have a short term base salary or draw and will soon shift to 100 percent commission

- If you are calling on smaller B2B accounts

- If others were terminated for low production numbers in the first six months

When You May Be OK with Pre-call Research

- If you are assigned large, high-visibility targets

- If you are expected to maintain and increase current account revenue within named accounts

- If your manager tells you that your new role is to meet-and-greet your account base over time rather than blast right into the market

- If the culture of your organization is "patient"

- If you receive a salary or nonrecoverable draw with minimal commission. This typically may indicate the organization isn't in a hurry to expand its net new business

- If the accounts you are required to pursue are Fortune 500 types you definitely will want to pre-research

The best approach for knowing when to research before a call may be a two-pronged strategy. If you need to show numbers quickly, start with *transactional* selling while you deploy a *relationship* strategy to reach key accounts outside your transactional base. The blended approach seems to work in most instances.

Relationship selling requires comprehensive research prior to contacting major accounts. When doing your research, one of the most significant pieces of information you should search for is the organization's *corporate initiative*. Since the business climate is constantly changing, so are the corporate initiatives of organizations. Thus, it is essential to not only research the company's product line and executive ranks, but also discover what their corporate initiatives currently are. The purpose of understanding corporate initiatives is to have a clear view of how you might support your contact in meeting their objectives. Just be prepared to "earn the right" to do business with the big accounts; this means winning a key account can typically take years. Remember, they aren't waiting around to meet you.

Relationship Development and Transactional Business

Once you have developed those key relationships, don't take them for granted. Stay in touch, be attentive, and consistently seek opportunities to be a resource to your client. It's important to maintain your initial contacts while you prospect within the account to maximize the total revenue potential for your firm. Take the opportunity to become a significant resource and a professional "consultant" to your client.

Once you have several key accounts producing, you definitely are in the catbird seat. However, having a handful of key accounts that are significant revenue producers doesn't rule out the need to drive net new business. The better strategy is to consistently be on the hunt and be aware of potential new opportunities not only within the account, but consistently seeking new logos outside of the account. Remember, your oil wells are always vulnerable; as a result, that makes you and your company vulnerable!

While you have been reading this book, odds are one or more of your competitors are strategizing to take over one of your best accounts. When you realize that everyone wants what you have, then you may stay on top of things better. You must protect what you have while you keep looking for new opportunities. It means driving net new business consistently. It may seem like it never ends, but if you look at your career as a journey and not a destination, you can get your head around what is necessary.

When Dialexis began, we were fortunate to have organizations such as DuPont, Apple, Gateway, and IKON engaged with us, as were many other major accounts. As time went on and we became comfortable, we got complacent and began to think the revenue would just keep coming in; after all, we were performing exceptionally well and had high-level contacts, so we discontinued driving net new business. We got lazy. Revenue continued for a while, and then some of our key oil wells went dry. We learned the hard way that our industry is often one of the early cut-points for organizations. As we said, in cases where we lost an oil well, it wasn't because we weren't performing at a high level or because of a dispute. It was for multiple reasons, all of which we didn't see coming. It represented another wake-up call along the course of our career. Now we continue to support our major account business while constantly stirring the pot for net new logos. We learned once again that when the big oil wells go dry, it can jolt a salesperson's revenue big-time, and, along the way, crush mindset. It is a humbling event. We decided we didn't want to go through that again. We know that if you are experienced and are reading this you will agree, because anyone who has been in selling for some time has lost a few oil wells and often without notice. If you are new in sales, take heed. If you don't believe your sales manager, take it from Dialexis: you can never stop prospecting for net new business; it's the DNA of a sales career.

When we were commercial real estate brokers, there was a competitor broker across the street that controlled a major account in our marketplace. We wanted to get that account, so we called on the company for years, attempting to gain control. All to no avail. The broker had a real lock on the business and a significant relationship with multiple decision makers. He no doubt deserved the loyalty he was receiving. We pursued the account for a few years until we thought it wasn't worth pursuing. Our view was, unless the broker dies, quits, or his contacts leave the company, there was little chance for us to get control. As a result, we moved on. Then, a couple of years later, we thought maybe it was time to check in with this account and make contact again, just for the heck of it. When we made the call, we found the same executives in place, but the broker who originally had control was no longer handling the account. When we asked what happened, they spoke very highly of the broker, but said they have a philosophy that they should change brokers every five years or so because they feel it's smart for them to see other perspectives. The broker had done nothing wrong, in fact he was one of the very best in the business; it was just the way that organization operated.

So, what's the lesson? *There is no certainty that the accounts we value most will stay with us.* Despite providing outstanding performance or even having a deep relationship, accounts may leave. Things happen. If you are in sales, remind yourself your career must be about continuous prospecting, always looking for net new accounts, not just prospecting within the account. The only insurance we have to protect our company and ourselves is to continue to look for new logos. We all want the answer to be different, but it's not. As a side note, we were angry at ourselves for not pursuing this account consistently. As we said, we didn't see a reason to continue to call on them since they seemed happy and satisfied. But if we had, who knows, this could have been our account for five years!

Determining How Many Dials a Day Are "Right"

How many new dials per day or per week are you required to make to satisfy your company? In our opinion, it's not the number of dials that's so important, it's the *quality*. If you are in this game called sales to make your life significantly better, have more spendable income, provide yourself with the opportunity to take vacations, enjoy life, have the ability to do what you want to for your family, or simply rise to the top of your game, then you can calculate the number of contacts you need to make to be successful. Notice we said the number of contacts vs. the number of dials. There are hundreds and thousands of salespeople that make dozens and dozens of dials per day, but it's not the number of dials that matters, it's the actual contacts with decision makers that matters. This is the first step to success. The next step is converting these contacts into appointments.

If you're making plenty of dials and struggling to make contact, then the SOAR formula is going to make your life a whole lot easier! In fact, you might think that the formula is too easy. Once you understand how to utilize SOAR, you will never go back to the old way of prospecting on the phone. You will find that driving net new business is a psychological and tactical game wrapped around powerful intention.

Back to the question of how many net dials a day we'd recommend. We can't suggest how many dials a day you should make, since it's up to you and your organization. With many Fortune 500 firms that SOAR, their salespeople may only make 10 or 15 net new dials per day. The primary reason is because when using SOAR, salespeople make contact at a high percentage rate, and as a result, the calls last longer.

The Bottom Line

How many new accounts do you ultimately want to own or have as your key accounts? How many do you presently have? Think of this as reengineering your career using a mathematical approach. How many potential clients do you need to contact in order to get an appointment? What is your closing ratio? How many potential presentations do you typically have to make to close a transaction? Do the math! When will you be making the money you would like to make and exceed the quota you are required to produce? Remember, if you use the SOAR formula, you can get to a decision maker or someone of high influence up to 90 percent of the time. On average, when dialing alone, if you fall below a contact rate of 70 percent you will need to get back to SOAR basics. The great news is that all of this is at your fingertips. All you have to do is take the steps. Your results are in your control!

The Best Days and Times to Prospect

We often are asked, "When is the best time to prospect?" or "Isn't it true that Mondays and Fridays are bad times to prospect?" We also hear, "Isn't it a fact that calling early in the morning or late after 5 p.m. is the best time?" Our answer to these questions is: anytime is a great time! The fact is, there is no bad time. The salespeople in the top 20 percent, the ones that are at the top of the leader board, will call without preconceived notions. They don't have rules or beliefs that there is some unique time of the day when it's a perfect time to drive net new business. They just get after it. Not getting started may be a *stall tactic* or represent *a block* you might have.

There really is no bad time to prospect in our belief because, if you have something of value to share with a potential client, then why would there be a bad time to present your products or services? Most businesses are looking for professionals to support them in navigating through the challenging waters of today's business world. Understand that you, your firm, and your offering can represent a critical resource to prospective clients.

Our suggestion to you is to let go of the belief that there is a "good" time to call and a "bad" time to call. Those are rules you may have put in your belief system based upon the experiences you have had, and, therefore, have made it the only way to approach your business. You may say, "Yes, but I have called on Monday mornings early and it has always caused problems for me," and our response to you would be that we understand that's what you are creating. It could be that you have a strong belief that calling on Monday mornings isn't a good time as a result, you create proof you are right by having problems on Mondays! We can tell you that, after decades of selling and training sales professionals, we have experienced no issues related to calling on a specific day or time . . . none! (Then again, we don't hold a belief that it's an issue.)

Prospecting on the Street vs. on the Phone: Which Is Best?

Here's how we see it: it certainly depends on what your company expects of you. You can make fewer calls on the street, but they can be more powerful. On the phone, you can reach more prospects, and if your techniques are sound, you may set more appointments. We have always said to salespeople that a mix usually works best. In the end, however, it's up to you, unless your organization has an expectation that you must do it a certain way. We have found that some salespeople love the streets, while others prefer the telephone. Who cares? It's the results that matter. Personally, we use both because we know both are powerful. We like what happens on the telephone because the results are fast and effective. Don't get us wrong: street prospecting is excellent, and we instruct SOAR *Streets* with many clients. SOAR is available in both formats: telephone and streets. However, this book is directed toward telephone prospecting for driving net new business. The thrill of making a live call in person as opposed to on the telephone can be an adrenaline rush. If you are making a live call on the telephone and you get stumped, you can always "hang up although you shouldn't," but when you are making a live, "in-person" call, you are in *real time* and there is no way out but to stay calm. Our view is that once you announce yourself and your firm, you should never hang up because you get nervous. Doing so damages the world of professional selling. As we have said, always leave the call better than you found it.

Relationship Prospecting vs. Transactional Prospecting

Here's one way to address the issue. If your responsibility is to drive revenue through "named" accounts, then relationship prospecting within the account may be your initial approach. There is always room to grow your account base outside of the account, so prospecting for additional new logos will support you in the long run.

If you are required to drive net new business immediately or you are trying to survive on 100 percent commission, then transactional prospecting is probably a necessity at the start. Jump on the transactional selling train big-time if you need to fill your pipeline quickly. But you should also plan to identify the relationship accounts you want to own and plan your strategy for contacting these accounts and ultimately controlling them.

The fact is, top sales professionals pursue both strategies at the same time, no matter if they have been given named accounts or not. You will get tired quickly and it will be a brutal way to make your numbers if you are simply focused on transactional prospecting. Imagine: over and over, year after year, banging on the phone or the streets to get a deal or find an opportunity. Now consider relationship selling. It may take longer, but the end result is you build an annuity account. So, while you are developing those key relationships, look under a million rocks for the immediate opportunities.

The Importance of Subconscious Messaging

In SOAR training, before our instructors ask salespeople to dial cold clients in class, they ask the caller what their *intent* is. The reply is often, "I'm going to *try* to get an appointment." When salespeople prepare to dial with a mindset of "I'm going to *try*" they are doomed. When you say "try," your subconscious says, "this may not work out," or, "sounds like this is a *try* call not a *make contact* call." Really, think about it: your subconscious is ready to deliver whatever you instruct it to deliver! If you want to make contact then tell your subconscious, "I'm going to make contact with the decision maker and get an appointment," not, "I'm going to *try* to make contact and try to get an appointment."

There is no "try." "Trying" is *attempting* to do something. In selling, we believe 100 percent there is only *we will*. Stop for a moment and think about the messages you have been giving your subconscious. Be committed. Shift your intention. You will be amazed at the change in your results when you implement the *mental game* outlined in SOAR.

Using your subconscious to support you also applies to any aspect of selling; when you are committed, you see the end result as you want it to be—you create an advantage that goes beyond the mechanics or technical knowledge. It's the power of using your beliefs to create the results you want, and beliefs equal mindset.

When there is a downturn in the economy, you have the opportunity to use positive messaging to move the ball forward. For example, we have many clients in the same industry, and even in the same regional locations, and yet we often hear the difference in their subconscious messaging. Many of these clients are extremely successful despite what may be happening in the market, while others are struggling. When we have a conversation with the successful firms, they acknowledge it's been a bigger challenge in this economy, but they believe the opportunities this business climate is presenting is amazing and, as a result, they are actually growing their business, hiring people, and expanding. To them, the market is abundant and the future is positive and exciting.

Organizations that see the economy as negative are downsizing and hunkering down as if there was a tornado or a hurricane coming. They don't see opportunities; they shift to a doom and gloom mindsets, and if you listen to how they speak you can "hear" what messages their subconscious are attached to. Our beliefs are very powerful that only we get to manage. If you listen to a corporation's messaging you will understand their thinking, and you will also discover why they may be in a downturn or an upturn . . . it's all based upon their thinking.

The Value of Paradigm Shifting

If you have been in sales several years and are doing well, you may be using the same strategy over and over, and although you are winning with it, it may be time to shift. Change is hard, but not changing is harder. The marketplace is constantly adjusting, and your customers' needs are changing just as rapidly. Being willing to shift your paradigm is vital. It is crucial for all of us, especially when we are in sales, whether you're striving for the top 20 percent+ or just wanting to ensure you stay there.

Let's say you are doing well and you are the big player in the office. Probably the last thing you want to hear is someone telling you it's time to change your strategy or consider a new selling approach, but it may be just the advice you need. A paradigm shift could be the best thing to do when you are ahead of the curve. That doesn't mean you should stop doing what's working; it simply means getting started on a *new way* to win while you maintain your current way. You may consider a new market to go after, a new offering, or a completely different strategy for driving revenue. Keep doing what has made you successful, just plan for your next *new* approach. Consider entertainers. They often stay on top due to their ability to shift their paradigm, to always change and create new material. They frequently call this reinventing themselves, and that is exactly what we are talking about. Shift the way you view your selling career, your products or services, and your approach. Even car manufacturers make constant changes each year to stay ahead of the competition. They don't discontinue what's working for them; rather, they continue to innovate, and that's how they stay ahead. If they don't, the competition will.

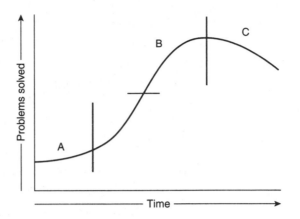

Figure BM-1A *Paradigm Curve*

A typical sales career follows the paradigm curve in Figure BM-1A.

A—You enter the first phase of your career. This is when you're new and still learning, not solving many problems.

B—In the B phase, your sales take off because you're solving lots of problems.

C—In the C phase, you failed to make a paradigm shift in time, and your productivity ends up in crisis because you stopped solving the more difficult problems.

When should you begin thinking about a paradigm shift? The answer is: when you are doing well and when you may not be doing well. Remember, when you are doing well you don't have to stop what you are doing. You don't have to drop your winning strategy, just *begin to look for new ways to create greater results to stay ahead of the curve.* As we have said, the competition is continually strategizing how to take your client. You never *own* the client. The client may love you, love your product, like your kids, have dinner with you, laugh at your jokes, maybe even attend the same church as you, but that doesn't mean you're safe. You can be dropped so fast you won't have time to go into shock. Your best defense is consistently reviewing your paradigm and continuing to drive net new logos. Think ahead of your competition. This is an area where you can become a "thought leader," someone that creates the curve.

A True Story

We once knew a top salesperson in the commercial furniture industry. This individual, like his competitors, would take clients to their local showroom to illustrate the newest concepts in furniture and office optimization. They would show the potential clients why they should consider using their products. Then came someone out of the box who was "creating the curve," that is, *the new paradigm*. This salesperson would meet with the prospect when a large furniture purchase was considered, but instead of taking the prospect through their showroom, he would meet the clients at their office and bring along an architect, a CPA, a tenant improvement contractor, and an executive assistant to keep a record of the meeting. Again, he didn't visit the showroom; he sat with his team in the client's boardroom and discussed the inplications of this type of purchase, including the advantages from a tax perspective, the advantages from a workflow perspective, and so on. He *created a new way of selling furniture*, a completely new concept in the world of commercial furniture sales. After this preliminary meeting, the potential client was impressed and ready to move further. Following the initial meeting, the salesperson would fly the prospective client and his team to the manufacturer's headquarters (on the company plane) to see how the furniture was made and how the manufacturer could custom-build to the client's requirements. This is shifting the paradigm in action! This participular salesperson created a new way of relating to key clients. The end result was that his selling approach became part of the *new norm* and he became more financially successful than any of his peers. Consider thinking outside of your existing paradigm.

20 Ways to Drive Net New Business in a Challenging Market

1. Find your vision/magnet—*then declare it.* This can be the most challenging part of creating the life you want, but it's worth the effort. Once you have your vision, your subconscious can begin working for you!

2. Associate with positive people—avoid *doom and gloom* conversations. Interestingly enough, negative people don't see themselves as negative. You will recognize them, however, so if they aren't positive contributors to your life, stay away.

3. Start prospecting again—realize it's not just for rookies. Protecting yourself by constantly finding net new business or new logos is key to having the life you want.

4. Understand that changing jobs may not be the answer—it rarely is. If you change companies you will most likely find similar issues at your new company. It's rarely the company that's the issue.

5. Realize that the economy is simply an obstacle waiting to be solved—*think positive* and use the obstacle to your advantage!

6. Intensify your work ethic and be excited about what you're up to—get busy, but stay close to your family, and remember: *you can have it all.*

7. Take 100 percent responsibility—you control your destiny. Don't become a victim.

8. Differentiate yourself—what do you personally have that sets you apart from the pack?

9. Avoid negative people—they are dream stealers, and their powers are strong. They can dim the spark of your vision.

10. Start positive self-talk—if you can think negative, you can think positive. Remember, your subconscious messaging is feeding you and your actions.

11. Acknowledge your skills—*you have the talent*. Get back to believing in yourself *again*. There is no one in the world like you!

12. Realize the competition is after your *loyal* accounts—protect your oil wells. Take the time to let them know you authentically care about them.

13. Get in earlier—put in a few hours on Saturday, but family first.

14. Requalify your pipeline—are they really deals?

15. Recognize your innate talent doesn't go away in tough times—your mindset does. Keep your eye on the target—don't get distracted.

16. Take it to the streets now and then—be aware; "see" what is happening in your marketplace. Opportunity may be right in front of you!

17. Commit to a *vision* meeting with yourself—spend "off time" strategizing. Think big, stretch your mind beyond where you are comfortable.

18. Ask someone who is winning how he or she is doing it—get humble, reach out, and be "real."

19. Get back to what got you to the top before—you did it once, and you can do it again.

20. Never give up—the pros always find ways, or they simply invent them. Reinvent yourself!

20 Wrap-Up Suggestions

Tip #1: Before you begin prospecting, have a "scrubbed" call list. (Chapter 2)

Tip #2: Have a compelling value statement. (Chapter 7)

Tip #3: Determine a realistic number of net new contacts you will commit to. (Chapter 2)

Tip #4: Get clear about your intention before dialing! (Chapter 3)

Tip #5: Raise your KWL antenna. (Chapter 5)

Tip #6: Less talk in the NIZ zone. (Chapter 5)

Tip #7: Be prepared for death questions. (Chapter 5)

Tip #8: Learn how to handle objections. (Chapter 9)

Tip #9: Increase your product knowledge. (Chapter 4)

Tip #10: Be prepared for the "send me something" request. (Chapter 10)

Tip #11: Use MOM to get callbacks, and remember to mark your cell phone. (Chapter 11)

Tip #12: Use SOAR in the social media world. (Chapter 12)

Tip #13: Understand the concept of "the chip" in the NIZ zone. (Chapter 5)

Tip #14: Use DiSC to make a personal connection. (Chapter 8)

Tip #15: Be sure your product knowledge is excellent. (Chapter 4)

Tip #16: Stay on the call: ride the bull 4 deep. (Chapter 6)

Tip #17: Get to the Power Zone. (Chapter 6)

Tip #18: Do not use "just let'm/let'r know" in the Power Zone, it's for the NIZ zone. (Chapter 6)

Tip #19: Understand the power of the EAP: respect is paramount. (Chapter 6)

Tip #20: Make it fun! (Chapter 3)

The following Figure BM-2 shows the complete FORMULA for making A SOAR CALL.

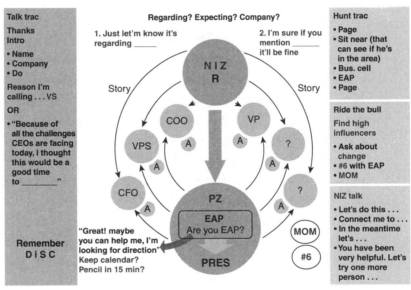

Figure BM-2 *Ride the Bull Map*

Summary Points for Following the Ride the Bull SOAR Call Map

1. Enter at the Receptionist level (The NIZ zone: "no information zone").

2. Ask for the president in the Power Zone (PZ).

3. Receptionist may ask you death questions: (Questions that if answered incorrectly will terminate the call.) Those questions are:
   - What is this *regarding?*
   - Is the president *expecting* your call?
   - What *company* are you with?
   - Is this a *sales* call?

4. You respond with:

   #1. *"Just let'm* (or if it's a female) *let'r know it's regarding [your name].*

   If the receptionist says, "will he/she know who you are?" You respond with:

   #2. *"I'm sure if you mention [your name], it'll be fine."*

   (Note: As unusual as it may seem, response #1 works because you are hitting the receptionist "chip" with the *"regarding"* word. It just works, you get passed through. When we suggest response #2 and state that it has *"always been fine,"* we know that to be true. The reasoning is that the receptionist generally won't mention your name to the president in the first place because it's just a "chip" question. (However, if you are calling a *very small* company the odds increase dramatically that the receptionist could mention who is calling, but we find it is always fine. In large firms it is rare, so why does a receptionist ask . . . because as we said they are chipped! Also, we know it will be fine because after thousands of live calls, it has always been fine. Can we say with 100 percent accuracy that it will always be fine? No, but we can say that the odds of it being fine are extremely high. In all the trainings we have personally conducted and our instructors have conducted, making live dials in class, it has always been fine.)

5. Move to the Hunt trac and follow the steps until you find the president or EAP
   - Page
   - Sit near

- Biz cell
- EAP
- Page

6. You consistently use the **NIZ talk tips** when Riding the Bull and directing the EAP
   - Let's do this . . . .
   - Let's try . . . .
   - Connect me to . . . .
   - You have been very helpful, let's try one more person . . . .

7. When you make contact with the decision maker, you use the **Talk Trac**:
   - Introduce yourself.
   - Tell the name of your company.
   - Tell what your company does. (Unless they would naturally know what your company does. Remember, unless your company has world class brand recognition the person you are speaking to may *not* know what your company does.)
   - Say, "the reason I'm calling is . . ." (The word *Reason* gets their attention.)

8. The reason you are calling can be said as:
   - "Because of all the change going on, I thought this would be a good time to [state your reason why it's a good time to introduce yourself, talk, etc. or insert your value statement]. OR you can say,
   - "Because of all the challenges CEOs are facing today, I thought this would be a good time to [state your reason why it's a good time to meet, talk, etc. or insert your value statement].

9. If you can't reach the president and you do reach the EAP, you can first confirm the person you are speaking to is the EAP by asking, "Are you the president's EAP? If the response is yes, then you would say,
   - "Great! Maybe you can help me? I am looking for direction." You would then introduce yourself and explain why you want

to speak to the president. The EAP may suggest you speak to someone else or suggest you leave a message. You then have several options, they are:

#1. Be transferred to the person the EAP *recommends* and upon making contact use the EAP's name as a reference (remember, the EAP has power).

#2. Leave a MOM for the president (Chapter 11).

#3. Ask the EAP for the president's business cell number. If you don't get it, then you can suggest you will hold while the EAP connects you to the cell.

#4. Ask the EAP if he/she keeps the president's calendar and would pencil in a 15-minute meeting with the president.

#5. If all else fails and you are in a local market, you can use #6 (see Chapter 10).

10. If no one is available in the Power Zone, you continue with the receptionist (stay on the bull and use the "hunt trac") and seek a high influencer to discover what *"change"* the organization may be going through. Then, follow up on a subsequent call or you can leave a MOM on the president's voice mail or cell phone if you have it.

Figure BM-3 shows the call process for getting a qualified appointment.

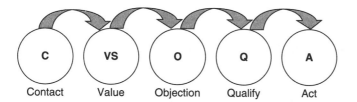

Figure BM-3 *Call Process for Getting a Qualified Appointment*

SOAR Call Stats: Throughout North America and Europe

The following SOAR call stats in Figure BM-4 have been recorded using thousands of live dials and averaged the stats made throughout North America and Europe. We advise you consider measuring your calls against these dial stats so you can compare your success with SOAR.

SOAR	Gross dials	N/A	Net dials	DM	HI	Appointments
SOAR running averages	100	40%	60	46	44	20%+

DM = Decision maker
HI = High influencer

Figure BM-4 *SOAR Calls Stats National Average*

Below in Figure BM-5 are the NIZ (No Information Zone) Zone receptionist responses, KWL (Keyword listening), and interpretations.

NIZ zone
Receptionist responses (KWL and interpretations)

1. I don't believe he is in . . . . (page) (cell)
2. I haven't seen him today . . . . (page) (cell)
3. He didn't answer . . . . (cell) (EAP)
4. She isn't available . . . (available . . . meaning?)
5. I wouldn't have his cell number . . . (who would?)
4. We don't give cell numbers out . . . (hold while you connect)
5. He doesn't have an assistant . . . (who handles . . . ?)
6. She's out of the country . . . (cell)
7. He has left for the day . . . (cell)
8. Would you like her voice mail . . . (MOM) (#6)

Figure BM-5 *NIZ Zone Receptionist Responses*

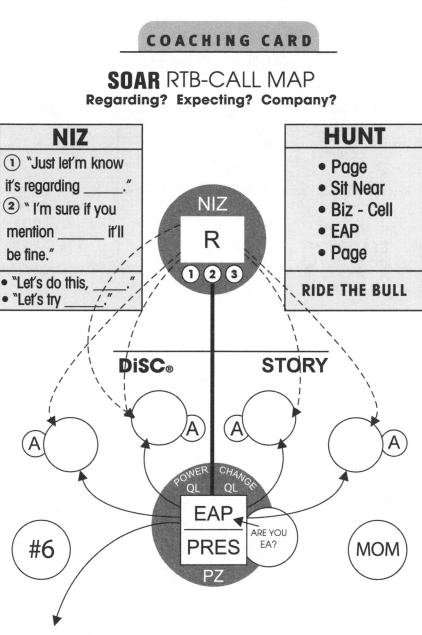

SOAR RTB-CALL MAP
Regarding? Expecting? Company?

NIZ

① "Just let'm know it's regarding _____."
② " I'm sure if you mention _____ it'll be fine."

- "Let's do this, _____."
- "Let's try _____."

HUNT

- Page
- Sit Near
- Biz - Cell
- EAP
- Page

RIDE THE BULL

NIZ

R

① ② ③

DiSC®

STORY

A

A

A

A

POWER CHANGE
QL   QL

EAP
PRES

ARE YOU EA?

PZ

#6

MOM

Great, MAYBE YOU CAN HELP ME . . . . looking for direction.

Do you keep ____'s calendar? Pencil in 20 min?

OPEN TO MEET?

Go to www.SOARSelling.com to download a personal copy of the SOAR Coaching Card.

SOAR TALK TRAC-MAP

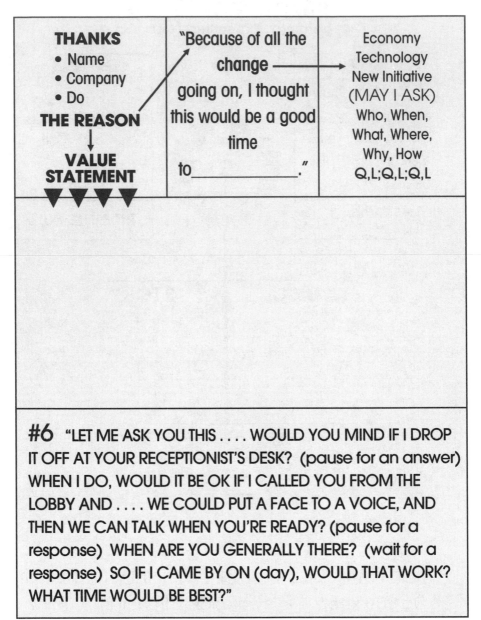

THANKS
- Name
- Company
- Do

THE REASON
↓
VALUE STATEMENT
▼▼▼▼

"Because of all the change ———— going on, I thought this would be a good time

to_____."

Economy
Technology
New Initiative
(MAY I ASK)
Who, When, What, Where, Why, How
Q,L;Q,L;Q,L

#6 "LET ME ASK YOU THIS . . . . WOULD YOU MIND IF I DROP IT OFF AT YOUR RECEPTIONIST'S DESK? (pause for an answer) WHEN I DO, WOULD IT BE OK IF I CALLED YOU FROM THE LOBBY AND . . . . WE COULD PUT A FACE TO A VOICE, AND THEN WE CAN TALK WHEN YOU'RE READY? (pause for a response) WHEN ARE YOU GENERALLY THERE? (wait for a response) SO IF I CAME BY ON (day), WOULD THAT WORK? WHAT TIME WOULD BE BEST?"

Go to www.SOARSelling.com to download a personal copy of the SOAR Coaching Card.

MOM OUTGOING

- "(prospect's name), THIS IS (your name) AND I'VE BEEN TRYING TO REACH YOU AND HAVEN'T HAD MUCH LUCK."
- "IF YOU COULD CALL ME BACK I WOULD APPRECIATE IT."
- "IT'S (time) RIGHT NOW AND I WILL BE AVAILABLE UNTIL AROUND (time)."
- "MY # IS 962.48 . . . . BETTER YET . . . . LET ME GIVE YOU MY DIRECT CELL #."
- "AGAIN, I WOULD APPRECIATE YOUR CALLBACK . . . ."
- "INCIDENTALLY, IF YOU NEED TO REACH ME TOMORROW THAT WILL WORK AS WELL."

MOM INCOMING

- "THANKS FOR RETURNING MY CALL (prospect's name)."
- "I KNOW MY MESSAGE MAY HAVE BEEN A LITTLE CONFUSING."
- "I WANTED TO REACH OUT TO YOU BECAUSE OF ALL THE CHANGE GOING ON IN TODAY'S MARKET."
- "I AM WITH (your company). WE ARE A _____ (tell what your company does)."
- "AND THE REASON I'M CALLING IS _____ (VS) (CI)."

Dialexis, inc.™

©2012 by Dialexis, inc.
All rights reserved. Not approved for duplication

www.SOARSelling.com
www.dialexis.com
1-800-98 PROFIT
1-800-987-7634

Go to www.SOARSelling.com to download a personal copy of the SOAR Coaching Card.

SOAR GLOSSARY OF TERMS

4 DEEP: Means to "stay on the bull" (the call) (see *Ride the Bull*) until you have reached your target. In the event your target isn't available, you would continue to *stay on the same call* until you reach your next target. If that person isn't available you continue the process until you have attempted to reach four people. Thus the term *4-deep* before you leave the call. In cases where a company is very small, this wouldn't apply; you may be able to only go 2-deep or there may be occasions where you release pursuit after 1-deep.

80/20: Pareto's Principle, or Pareto's Law as it is sometimes called, represents the concept that 20 percent of something always is responsible for 80 percent of the results; commonly referred to as the **80/20 Rule**.

A + P = E: Attitude + Performance = Employability. A simple formula that implies that Attitude without Performance is not acceptable and Performance without a positive Attitude is also not acceptable. Employability requires both.

APPOINTMENT: A set date and time.

BTN + L: Refers to the old way of prospecting "by the numbers + luck" (vs. the new SOAR method).

BUNDLING: Asking qualifying questions without solving each question or objection as they are given. Bundle the objections until you believe you have them all . . . then solve.

BUSINESS CELL: Same as a regular cell phone, but asking for the business cell implies it's not the personal cell.

CANOE THEORY: A published leadership book by David & Marhnelle Hibbard and Jack Stockman, PhD, *The Canoe Theory* describes how any organization can work as a powerful team.

CHANGE: When calling, you may ask about "change" since all companies are going through *change* and we know that *change* often precipitates need.

CHIP: A way of saying that receptionists are trained from day one to ask callers certain questions, referred in SOAR as the three "death questions." After time on the job, receptionists may still ask those death questions without really caring if they get the answer because they are just "chip" questions that no longer have meaning. Answering those questions incorrectly will often lead to the death of the call.

CONTACT: Reaching a Decision Maker (DM) or High Influencer (HI). *See "in rate."*

CP + D = VS: A formula for creating a value statement. Client Pain + Differentiator = Value Statement.

DEATH QUESTIONS: Questions the receptionist asks in the NIZ zone that, when answered incorrectly, often lead to call termination *("what is this regarding?" "is he/she expecting your call?" "is this a sales call?" and "what company are you with?")*

DEMAND GENERATION: Prospecting—driving new business.

DIALS: Each time you attempt to make a call it counts as a gross dial. (It does not imply that the organization you are calling answered.)

DiSC®: A behavioral profile system published by Inscape Publishing and used to discover individual behavior in a given environment.

DM: Decision Maker.

DOT: An example used in SOAR—the accumulation of all your knowledge to date from which you make all your decisions, that is your *dot*.

DREAM: Your vision, will, goal, "magnet" . . . essentially, what it is that you most want.

EAP: Executive assistant to the president.

FAILURE RATE: A DM/HI contact rate using SOAR that is below 70 percent.

FOUNDATIONS OF ACHIEVEMENT: The four basic Dialexis discoveries to success.

GROSS DIALS: The number of attempted dials/calls made before N/As are taken out. *See N/A.*

HI: High Influencer (generally a VP, C-level contact, or a specific declared influencer in the organization that can impact your ability to get an appointment, provide reliable information, or lead you to a successful transaction.

IN RATE: Represents the percentage (%) of contact rate with DM and HI.

KWL: Keyword Listening.

L + AWAE = E: Loyalty + A Well Articulated Excuse = Employment. *(This should not be the case!)*

MAGNET: Vision, goal, objective; your declaration of intention to achieve something.

MINDSET: definition, Merriam-Webster dictionary: *a mental attitude or inclination; a fixed state of mind; a particular way of thinking: a person's attitude or set of opinions about something.*

MOM: Message of Mystery.

N/A: A *Non-Applicable* call. That is, a call that does not count because of one of the following: **1.** wrong number, **2.** no answer, **3.** lost in technology and can't get back to the operator, **4.** "rode the bull" four times and hung up due to the operator becoming annoyed or, **5.** no one was in that day.

NEC: No Excuse Commitment.

NET DIALS: The number of calls/dials less N/As. *See N/A.*

NET NEW CALLS: Prospecting calls that represent *new business* rather than existing business. *See new logos.*

NEW LOGOS: Prospecting for *new logos* implies you are prospecting for business that is outside of existing companies you may have. A new logo would be an entirely new company you have contacted.

NIZ ZONE: The *No Information Zone* where the receptionist resides.

OIL WELLS: An acronym used for *major accounts.*

PARADIGM: The rules you use to define how you run your life, business, or anything you have fallen into a pattern on. A paradigm shift is when you change the rules of your paradigm fundamentally.

PASSION/WILL: Your goal, vision, or dream. It's what you stand for or may have declared as your intention to achieve.

PC + KWL = Q: A qualifying formula: Percent of Chance + Keyword Listening = Qualifying.

PICK THE BONES: Find out about *change* when reaching the EAP, HI, or DM prior to transferring.

PK: Product knowledge.

POWER ZONE: The area where the president and EAP reside.

Q,L;Q,L;Q,L: Question, listen; question, listen; question, listen.

RIDE THE BULL: Stay on the call until you have attempted to talk to one person out of four attempts.

SIT NEAR: Asking the receptionist for a person who "sits near" your desired target who may be able to *see* if he or she is in the area.

SMS: "Send me something." A common response received on a new prospecting call.

SOAR: Surge Of Accelerating Revenue.

SOAR WORLD AVERAGES: The average contact rate and appointment rate that the SOAR program has recorded after thousands of *cold* calls reported to Dialexis or as measured in classroom training. The contact rate should never fall below 70 percent and should be consistently at 80 to 90 percent of every net dial. Decision Makers are running at, over, and below 46 percent and High Influencers are recording an average of 44 percent.

STORY: Explaining your previous path of activity to a secondary contact during live calling.

STORY: *See dot.*

THE BEACH: An analogy of a place to think. The park, your den, the lake, and so forth, could all be considered *the beach.*

TOP 20 percent+: Becoming successful by attaining the top 20 percent and more in your rankings within the company. (The "+" implies higher than 20 percent.)

VALUE STATEMENT: What you say to the client upon contact on a new call in the first 20+/− seconds that creates interest.

$$R + CI + D = VS$$
or
$$P + D = VS$$

VS: *See Value statement.*

INDEX

ABOUT THE AUTHORS

David Hibbard has over 25 years' experience in the sales industry. As cofounder of Dialexis, an industry leading sales training organization that creates high-producing sales leaders, he trains professionals in a variety of industries at companies such as Cisco, Apple, AT&T, Oracle, and Toshiba. By presenting the proven and top performing SOAR Selling process, David empowers individuals and businesses to be more profitable, more successful, and marketplace leaders while maintaining integrity and trust.

David's corporate career began at Procter and Gamble, where he developed the formal elements of his talent. He then spent 18 years in the highly competitive commercial real estate industry. As a result of his sales skills, determination, and street savvy, he was honored as the "Number-One Rookie" in the country and the "Number-One Broker" in one of the most competitive brokerage operations in the United States. After achieving exceptional success brokering, David accepted a Leadership role at Grubb and Ellis, where he was one of the leading trainers for all Grubb & Ellis incoming broker candidates.

David is the coauthor of *The Canoe Theory: A Business Success Strategy for Leaders and Associates.* His goal is to support businesses and individuals to reach the top 20 percent+ in sales performance.

Marhnelle Hibbard has over 20 years' experience in sales and personal development. As cofounder of Dialexis, she is a personal leadership coach and delivers keynotes and workshops on leadership and sales. A sought-after speaker, her expertise and strategies have helped organizations such as DuPont, Herman Miller, Steelcase, Wells Fargo, BRE and other executives throughout the United Sates to grow their business, enhance team results, and reach new levels of sales success.

Marhnelle began her professional career as one of the few women in Commercial Real Estate brokerage and Commercial Real Estate development. During her 17 years marketing major development projects throughout California, she gained many of the experiences she relies upon to deliver the intensity of her message.

Marhnelle gained national recognition by authoring an internationally distributed Personal Development Program for women. In addition, she coauthored a highly acclaimed leadership book, *The Canoe Theory: A Business Success Strategy for Leaders and Associates.* Her passion is to partner and work with individuals and leaders who are coachable and committed to a higher platform of success.

Now that you've finished the book SOAR Selling, there's more! Visit our website at www.soarselling.com to learn more about how the SOAR formula creates success and explore the following topics in-depth:

- SOAR Corporate (For organizations with 20+ sales people)
- SOAR Leadership (Support your leaders in making Net New Business a reality)
- SOAR Measurement (Accountability – ROI formula)
- SOAR Train the Trainer (For large enterprise sales teams)
- SOAR Coaching (Find a coach that will support you in reaching your vision and goals)
- SOAR Online (Support your career with additional SOAR practices and SOAR live dial)
- SOAR Blitz (Focused demand generation day to increase revenue and new business)
- SOAR *Live* (SOAR instruction for individuals or organizations with small sales teams)

Enter the code **7627 (SOAR)** on our website to download a formatted *Ride the Bull* Coaching Card and preview a SOAR live dial.

Dialexis Overview

Dialexis has been dedicated to improving the results of organizations and individuals for over two decades. The company is committed to support those seeking high impact results because we believe it's possible. Corporate success and personal satisfaction do not oppose each other. Over the past 24 years, our goal has been focused on enhancing the lives of those that seek more and are looking to take their professional and personal growth to the highest level.

Our purpose is to support every individual in having the life they want through providing a resource of developmental instruction in the areas of sales, leadership, coaching and large group speaking. Since 1988, Dialexis has been retained to support a wide range of industries, including computer manufacturing, commercial furniture, entertainment, finance, banking, technology, insurance, commercial real estate, gaming, medical research, sports apparel, and general manufacturing industries throughout North America and Europe. Additionally, Dialexis has worked hand-in-hand with key sales professionals and leadership executives in a coaching capacity, yielding exceptional ROI.

Additional Dialexis Offerings

SOAR Selling (*Surge Of Accelerating Revenue*)

The Proven Method for Reaching Decision Makers

This measurable demand generation program is the most effective new business development strategy in the marketplace! It has been utilized by numerous Fortune 500 companies with a high rate of success. Salespeople walk out of the SOAR program with a formula for increasing appointments with decision makers and high influencers and do so with a first time contact rate of up to 90 percent. Additionally, SOAR is distinguished by the fact that it is measureable, provides for accountability and has delivered a 200–2000 percent ROI in as little as 12 weeks. The program is broken into powerful components, including a leadership segment, and involves live dialing in-class for sales participants.

Web-Based Learning

All material presented during the Webinar has been derived from the *real world* of selling. Nothing is made up; all training has been created from the field of professional selling. The Webinar material is presented powerfully and applies to salespeople with any level of experience, from beginner to experienced. Attendees realize immense take-away value using a platform that it is *fast, economical, and effective.*

Value Statement Development

What to Say On a Prospecting Call in the First 30 Seconds

Value Statement development focuses on the creation of compelling and powerful value statements for an organization's sales teams. The program is delivered in a workshop format with pre-research that allows the Dialexis instructor to develop the value statements that are in line with what the organization brings to the market. The instruction provides guidance on what to say in the first 30 seconds of a net new dial that is compelling enough for the prospect to engage in conversation, ask questions, or set an appointment. A powerful value statement allows a salesperson the opportunity to initiate immediate interest when making contact with a prospect. Knowing what to say leads to an opportunity for deeper discovery, and, in turn, the chance to set more qualified appointments. Dialexis will create a master *value statement* product following the program and provide it to the organization for reproduction and delivery to the sales teams.

Excellence In Leadership (EIL)

Transformational Aspects of Leadership

Excellence In Leadership provides participants with the opportunity to discover fundamental distinctions pertaining to what it means to lead. Managers move from a desire to "control" things into the domain of creating new results, regardless of current circumstances. Attendees create a leadership vision and be provided strategies for delivering that vision to the organization. The training provides a platform for participants to discover hidden *blind spots* that may be preventing the opportunity for exceptional leadership.

Leadership Mechanics
Tactical Aspects Of Leadership
This leadership offering is focused strictly on the *mechanics* or *tactics* a leader requires to develop an organization. It provides the "tools" most Dialexis clients say their management team is requesting. The program looks at the *how to* of developing a team and culture as well as the construction and delivery of a leader's vision. Key areas of focus are: how to *find*, *interview* and *get* candidates to join the organization, how to motivate and retain talent, how to deal with internal conflict, techniques for holding teams accountable, how to develop marketplace image, how to create "on target" internal training, and the importance of energizing teams. *Leadership Mechanics* provides an excellent support arm to the Excellence In Leadership format.

Foundations of Achievement: A Keynote Speaking Event
Successfully hitting the mark during a keynote is a Dialexis constant. A Dialexis keynote address is delivered with passion, conviction, and energy, creating a memorable event for all participants. Dialexis recognizes that an entertaining delivery without substance is not worthy of a high-performance result. Dialexis has the reputation of being the best when it comes to delivering high content along with strong take-away value. The program will not only inspire attendees to achieve greater results, but also provide key strategies for tactical performance. Many presentations are headlined as "motivational;" *Foundations of Achievement* offers more. Dialexis suggests attendees bring pen and paper and be positioned to learn and apply the strategies delivered upon return to their day-to-day challenges.

Performance Coaching
Top performers reach peak performance with a coach. The majority of professional athletes or high performing individuals retain a coach. A high performance coach can make the difference in winning due

to a coach's unique ability to discover tactical or transformational opportunities that may have been undiscovered, preventing optimum performance. Dialexis has been engaged in coaching top professionals with their personal and corporate goals for over two decades. Dialexis Coaching was developed specifically to support individuals or groups to go beyond what they may have thought possible. Through collaboration and conversation, the Dialexis coach will uncover limiting beliefs that often prevent exceptional performance. This type of coaching is often best for those that have achieved a unique level of success, but who are looking to go even further. Dialexis seeks individuals that have made a decision to play *all in*.

For more information, please contact Dialexis at: 1-800-98PROFIT (1800-987-7634)